To the Reader:

This is a book that's not about one thing, such as old stories, or spirituality, or how to think, or how to feel better.

This is my life, ninety-one years of it. It is what I was and what I have become—my ancestral roots, the family I grew up with, the family I nourished, the places that nourished me; it is what I explored—how I became a contemplative, the music I heard, the visions I saw, what I dreamed, how I've lived as a woman during nine decades of this evolution of our culture. It is about dying—giving up embodied spirit—which, like art and music, is all at once wholly sensuous, physical, and spiritual.

I have written this remembrance like music, a conversation of ideas, fragments, little flashes of illumination—juxtaposed, alluded to, reverberating, entangled, intertwining like counterpoint, always changing—heard in new context with richer meaning, transformed.

It is a story-poem, using stories the way poets use words.

It is about the way of the sacred ordinary. It is about how I loved. It is about how I love.

Skip what you will. Don't agree with me. Go look for yourself. Live your own sacred ordinary.

Remember. Remember who you are.

Urashan

THE
SACRED
ORDINARY

THE ODYSSEY OF A
NINETY-ONE-YEAR-OLD
CONTEMPLATIVE

URASHAN

Also by Urashan

Tropos: The Sacred Wheel
A mythic dance-opera

Cover, book design, and editing by Pollock Editorial Services (jspollock.com)
Cover photograph "Ave Maris Stella" © 2019 by John Schelling Pollock
Back matter photographs are from Urashan's collection, except photographs
on pp 413-415 and 429-435 © John Schelling Pollock (juanarto.com)
Back page photo (p 437)—representing the bodhisattvas on p 335—
© Anne Whitehurst (flickr.com/photos/31420281@N03)

Published by Maris Stella Press
18336 Aurora Ave N, Ste 105, Unit 55143, Shoreline, WA 98133
info@marisstellapress.com
urashan.com and marisstellapress.com

FIRST EDITION - 7

ISBN: 978-0-57-854685-8

Maris Stella Press

In gratitude to that anonymous

fourteenth-century mystic who wrote

The Cloude of Unknowyng

NOW

9

THEN

43

FOREVER

259

The Goddess was bored.

There She was, the All-in-All, in the radiance of Her glory, in the primordial void, all-seeing, all-knowing, all-powerful, eternal, everywhere ablaze with infinite possibility, yet empty of all form or particularity. *Let's get some action here*, She thought, *I want to experience other.*

And so She did.

And so She does. The fire of Her love pours forth the cosmos. All being, consciousness, energy, matter—that which evolves into stardust and galaxies and planets, with rocks and mountains and oceans and every imaginable living being—all saying you, me; here, there; now, then; change; time; matter. It's all Goddess, everywhere: within, without. Everything that happens is the result of one chunk of divine energy interacting with another.

We are how the Goddess experiences other. And it's all sacred.

There is a more succinct story: God spoke.

NOW

It is hard to explain the contemplative life:

So what are you doing?

Restoring the beauty of the universe.

Oh.

I live at the beach now, in a home I've named *Maris Stella: Star of the Sea.*

I've returned to my home view: Puget Sound and its great tides, its ever-shifting sands and tide pools; the herons and eagles, the shrieking gulls and terns, the shy loons and the traveling geese; the orcas and salmon; the looming presence of the snow-capped mountains; the old familiar lighthouse flashing its warning, three-by-three, through the night; and the soft, silver rain—tangible, intimate.

Every morning I am quickened to life by the flight of birds—brants, gulls, terns—flashing across the water; the ever-changing tidescape; the early morning sun, should there be any, picking out the foothills of the Olympics, those great western mountains.

At sundown, stepping onto the deck, I sing the *Ave Maris Stella,* to honor the Goddess, to show gratitude for my life, and for the sheer love of it all. That ancient hymn to the Mother of us all has been sung for well over a thousand years now. All I know are the Latin words; I don't know if anyone even knows the archaic words.

Sometimes Venus—that other Star of the Sea, Portal to Heaven, the embodiment of all beauty—is there at sunset, ablaze next to the new moon; sometimes her orbit takes her to the far side of the sun, obscure, traveling toward dawn.

I am an old woman, remembering. The laughter of little children goes with me everywhere: they are playing in my back yard, they dance on the beach, always flickering just out of sight, like the almost-seen stars at twilight.

I've always wanted an abundance of life, an abundance of children to love. When I was sixteen, I said I wanted eight children, and that is what came about. They are so vibrant, so beautiful!

I am well-loved; they are my tomorrow.

I think back to the first time here at this island that I can remember. I am five and I have just learned to print my name. I clamber over the logs up by the old steamer dock, next to the derelict general store, and find a hard, damp stretch of good gray-brown sand for my name. I can remember the feel of my forefinger tracing hard through the resisting marvelous stuff. I was wearing blue gingham.

Here the stars look right; everything *feels* right.

This is my endgame. I will die here.

The Olympics are magnificent this morning,
loaded with snow all down the foothills,
mist rising out of Hood Canal.

didn't expect to live here now. My meager retirement funds didn't stretch to a house at the beach.

Then something I never remotely imagined happened: Victoria died. My brother Ken's daughter, my niece. An only child, never married, she'd lived alone for many years since her parents' deaths. Eccentric, too proud to let anyone know she couldn't take care of her house or even her own needs, one day she simply curled up at the foot of the stairs and died. I was one of her heirs.

At about the same time, Stan and Sue Pocock wanted to sell this place. They loved this house and were glad to find someone who would love and respect its beauty. Stan and I had known each other as children when we all lived in Laurelhurst in Seattle, Ken and Stan best friends. And so it was a happy transaction accompanied by rich, shared remembrance.

It's a bittersweet gratitude at the heart of my coming to this place, my final home, in this way.

I remember Victoria here—tall and lovely, and so fair, laughing, striding down this beach on a fine, bright day—happy.

Here on Whidbey Island I feel close to primal mind. Primal mind—deeper than civilized mind—not something special only to tribal and indigenous people, but deep within everyone. Intuitive, heart-rich, it is the source of achingly beautiful music and art, the wellspring of compassion and justice, that true justice which is mercy. It is rooted deep, deeper than nations and laws and hierarchy, deeper than gender, deeper even than species.

This is deep home.

What I love, what I know, how I think now, is not how I was brought up. I didn't get the familiar, intellectual, academic life I'd planned; the world certainly didn't work the way I thought it should. So I took a closer look. My heart was deeper than I knew. My curiosity was intense; I somehow found the courage to explore the unknown.

I grew up gently Protestant, more about conscience than fear. In college I sang with the Unitarians, learned pacifism and service from Quakers, seasoning it all with a touch of the pagan and the deep love of place.

Then I came back from a year in Italy, jolted by the knowledge that people there knew something I didn't, that let them turn white stone into the warmth of living flesh, the earth of brick and tile into the magnificence of a cathedral's huge dome—yet so delicate in the mists coming down from the Tuscan hills. Nothing puritanical here: body matters. The material grounds vision; beauty trumps duty and fear.

It was the beauty that gave me the courage.

Maris Stella: a house of joy, a place for contemplation. Casual, elegant, simple, it is all about the sea, the mountains, water, light. Hexagons, angles, sharp corners, tilted roofs, glass everywhere looking out. Strong intersecting lines, great black beams, open space with no ceilings, stone tile. And cedar! Cedar everywhere: old cedar in the original great room, the cedar that was chosen for the Pocock racing shells in the new wing.

Cedar is the main color, with accents of dark orange-red, Chinese red, deep peacock, indigo, purple, and deep pansy. The mats are straw, the muslin unbleached, there's gold in one of the rugs; all with strongly contrasting espresso-black beams, black stove, and black grand piano. The shiny, white heat pumps, the refrigerator, glare sharply—I don't like them.

Everyone likes my new propane stove. It suits this place—a combination of stark Japanese contrasts and simplicity in a relaxed, well-loved beach house. I got it to replace the work-intensive wood stove. I am old now, I no longer have it in me to haul wood and clean out ashes, but I have the joy of nostalgia, of remembered fires.

Living here, in this amazing, extravagantly beautiful house, I feel wild, full, happy. This is not a box. The space here is organic, always in motion, moving through the rafters, washing through the open ceilings, collecting in bright, acute corners. Outside, light sloshes over the beams, pours over the shorter roof, swirls around the deck, meets its own reflection in one of the high windows, and from there, moves over the full sea, to the far horizon with its entire mountain range and full-soaring galactic sky.

Enchanted by light!

Silence is elusive.

I meditate on the sound of the
hypnotic sea rote, the whispering
wind; this morning, the high fluting
of an eagle.

What to call a pathless journey
with no destination, a passage
through time without particular
location, a non-journey that is
simply compassionate being?

Slouching toward Zen?

I live what is euphemistically called alone. This place is more like a do-it-yourself bed-and-breakfast than the simple shelter of a contemplative. The ratcatcher, the electrician, the groundskeeper, the water pump guy, my caregivers and drivers, my friends, and all my numerous family—nearly every day, someone drops in.

How to maintain simplicity? Eight or ten people cooked here last week. They brought food, flowers, cleaning gear. They rearranged the refrigerator, drawers, shelves, even the garbage and recycling system. Tall people put things where I can't reach them. Someone needed a meatloaf pan, a cookie sheet, a large salad bowl, a juicer. I have acquired large pots, lots of knives, vases, and pitchers. I keep several can openers in a drawer near the stove, hoping they don't all wander away.

I've lost no small measure of control over my life. However, I am firm about making sure people return keys and flashlights to their designated emergency stations. I know where the blankets are; I keep my bottled water supply replenished, my cell phone charged and nearby.

But never mind the chaos. All I have to do to restore myself to simple happiness and peace is to raise my eyes to the sea, the sky, the mountains, and I am lost in glory.

I used to go out on black starry nights and rejoice that I could see the stars, thinking they couldn't know I was here. Now I think otherwise. Of course they know I am here. The cosmos knows itself; it is alive.

I think we have been looking at things the wrong way, asking the wrong questions for many centuries, seduced by time's arrow, dazzled into blindness by the wonders of mathematics, physics, biology. But we are not unique and howlingly lonely beings, some accidental turn of biology, an anomaly of this watery, blue planet—we are part of all the energy of the universe. This stuff we think we're looking out at isn't *out there;* we are in the midst of it; we *are* the stuff.

Anywhere in time there is all this matter and energy; anywhere out of time, in the vast, unimaginable realm of eternity, there is still all this being. And it didn't just happen once. Being is constantly arising—luminous, sacred, alive—constantly providing us with our vitality, our ground, our commonplace.

A surfeit of being.

Up at the crack of dawn.

That is, ten to eight.

There is a magical moment frozen in my memory when the family was happy, when we all loved each other. We didn't yet know how searing adolescence could be, how all of us would be challenged by questions of class and race and of the nature of the humanity of women. It was a half-century ago, before the Vietnam War harrowed us to pieces, before St. Mary's College fell into so much blame and hatred, before we felt betrayed by all of our social institutions: church, school, government, before the backlash of anger and depression and too much alcohol, before we learned that truth was different from what we'd thought. We were about to be hit by whirlwinds and earthquakes. But for a little time, as we were about to celebrate Christmas, we were happy.

Ardent Christians then, followers of the down-to-earth Catholic Worker movement, Alan and I, in preparation for Christ's birthday, were about to observe Advent with our children. This meant a somber month of quiet waiting: praying, reading, singing, doing these things together. I loved the music and ritual of the liturgy—Gregorian chants with their medieval modes, the change of colors according to the seasons—purple for Advent—and I wanted to get it right.

We set up the crèche, minus the Babe, whom we were awaiting, of course, come midnight on Christmas Eve. We had a splendid Advent calendar and the sweet-smelling Advent wreath made of fresh evergreens, with its four candles—three purple, one rose—for each of the weeks leading up to Christmas Day. The rose candle was for the third Sunday, when the chosen verse said, "Rejoice, He is coming." Every evening we would light the appropriate candles, move the far-off wise men with their camels a little closer to the stable, adjust the herald angel, perhaps move the sheep and donkey around a little, and open one more little door on the calendar to see what tiny picture was inside, counting down the days until Christmas. We didn't put up the tree, with its lights and decorations, until Christmas Eve.

Alan, in his lovely rich voice, would read the liturgical verse for the day, and we would sing: "I Wonder as I Wander Out Under the Sky," and "O Come, O Come, Emmanuel," and other encouraging songs, getting ready to burst forth with the great Alleluias of Christmastime.

One year an enterprising writer for our local paper thought it would make a good story to feature the Christmas festivities of the family of St. Mary's College's vice president. So there we all are, so full of hope and glory—Alan and I with our children, Kate, Martha, Thomas, Sarah, John, Jacob, Michael, and David—gathered around my grandmother's old oak table, with the Advent wreath, candles ablaze, still singing our hearts out on that yellowed newspaper now more than five decades old.

Tonight is the new moon, invisible,
feasted with foghorns and rolling
surf and sharp little swirls of
dancing rain.

When did we first understand death? That everyone dies? When did we begin to imagine our own death? Was there awe? Curiosity? Bone-deep fear? What was it like when Eden shattered?

I slide back through time, before the industrial age, before the great shift to agriculture, to the time when we first began realizing death took away someone we loved. What was it like, watching someone you loved die? Was that when we began to develop an awareness of ourselves as separate from one another? Was that when all the separation began?

We remembered. We knew.

Knowing separation, we were learning to name, to count. We began to bury the dead, to bury them with ceremony. We developed that way of communicating that speaks with emotions and holistic knowing; we began to make art. We danced, we sang our stories, we learned to make flutes and drums. We put our handprints on the walls of our caves and painted them with pictures of the animals we hunted and killed. We were learning about time, watching the cycles of the moon, the seasons written in the stars.

We were saying, "I am. I am. Remember me."

Art is the utterance of the whole person: embodied emotions compounded by intellect and memory. Art is music, the utterance of time; it is the language of the heart, the language of illumination; it is poetry. Art becomes a gift of consolation as we endure the agony of separation.

Much, much later, the poet, remembering, says, "Death is the mother of beauty."

I used to say I did the work of the contemplative, but that is not true. It is not work. I don't *do* anything; I *be* everything.

I have chosen to live as a contemplative in the midst of life. I have not sought out a monastery. I have not followed any particular religion. I am exploring what it means to *be*.

It is challenging, deeply satisfying, often painful. I watch the sacred reveal itself in every aspect of ordinary living.

Contemplation is simply paying attention.

Philosophy—the love of wisdom—should be like good fiction, revealing, rather than explaining; but philosophers often seem separated, apart, seeking an exalted purity.

I am a thinker. The word *philosopher* carries too much freight; it is too pretentious for what I do—a sharing of vision, how I see things, not a laying down of absolutes. I am not continuing in the tradition of those exalted men who wrote from the unexamined security of an entrenched male culture and saw no need to include women in their considerations, and who for the most part supposed women incapable of rational thought and unworthy of education.

Meaning, for me, as a woman, is always embedded, enmeshed in the lives of others: I learn from the love of others; I write, like Emily Dickinson, in fragments.

O master, bless me, that I may
reconnect the mother voidness
and the son awareness.

There it all is, embedded in the ancient
Tibetan indigenous tradition called Bön.

This time of my life, this contemplation, this *being*, is far harder than I had imagined. My very self has changed, *is* changing, as has/is my relationship to everything.

For certain, my glory days are over, the lush, rich days of my summer have ended and all the children have gone. I feel as though I am resting on the node of some immense vibrating string. Everything around me is intensely alive; I am quiet—breathing deeply, watching.

It has been a long, long time since I've sat before hundreds of people and shared my heart's music or awakened a solitary student to music's blazing mystery. I no longer cook dinner for ten every night, nor host the great celebrations. It's a lifetime since I have nursed a marvelous new baby to bliss.

My dearest friends have slipped away one by one, like falling stars. I don't go out much. I almost never go off-island.

Yet it is an oddly vibrant, radiant time. The mysteries of the soul draw me deep into an inner world: contemplative, solitary, mystical.

I am sharply aware of the light everywhere, of birdsong, of the eagle soaring upward past the black firs, of the spicy scent of fallen apples, sparkling red on the damp, new autumn grass, of the being of everything, of the strange existence of my own flesh.

The wheel turns. My *self*, this awareness of embodied spirit, has softened. The question, *Who am I?* — so urgent in youth and in the upheavals of middle age — has become irrelevant; I am way past that.

With softer edges, I become deeply compassionate, radiant. I manifest peace, breathing deeply of each morning's sweet freshness. I am filled with an abundance of grace. No, I *am* grace, incarnate.

It is strange, this embodiment of spirit, a paradoxical merging of time and timelessness. Undifferentiated in infancy, we learn to objectify; we learn *I* and *it*. We think of the body as separate; we do things *to* it; we avoid pain. Sometimes our bodies feel like limitations or even betrayals. Sometimes we separate out our souls, imagining them to be objects in this odd container, this material body.

Yet, living, we are whole, a unity that cannot be broken or divided. This elegant simplicity is rooted to the core in nature, a unity, not of coming together, but of never having been torn apart.

Just as I find some understanding of this unity, this embodiment of spirit, I must let it go. Nearing the end, my spirit loosens its connection: senses diminish, appetites dwindle; to be touched feels like burning. My soul, my embodied spirit—evanescent, luminous, shimmering with transparency—is simply dissipating.

I am being drawn quietly toward eternity and the final transfiguration, the great un-naming of death.

The paleontologist, becoming old, writes about how light is the source of everything.

The storyteller, also old, describes the brilliant light that shines from all the tiny golden Tarot figures dancing the sacred mysteries, the universe in microcosm.

The Tibetan lama, not yet old, speaks of the inseparability of emptiness and light.

I love these last days of autumn. It is a time for dreaming and remembering, going deep within, deep into the earth, deep into the past, and from that dark quiet, looking up to the forever stars, waiting, hoping.

The sacred geometry is at work. Late this afternoon we start a journey of renewal—winter begins.

Once, when I was learning how to live by myself, driving south after a visit with friends in Oregon, I stopped at a dark, rocky beach near Crescent City to watch the rising of the winter solstice sun.

I became filled with the pounding rhythm of that morning surf and the hope that lay in that pallid light:

> Pale ruby solstice sea
>   greets the sun. Thin, wan light
>   thunders up the southern quarter
>   scatters mists and melts
>   the freezing rime.
>
> Quiet heart smolders in her Stonehenge
>   dream 'til sun cradles lightless moon,
>   pulls the heavy ocean mantle over
>   granite earth in ancient
>   sure embrace.
>
> And then begins the reaching soul to soul,
>   the stir of living things. Cast off
>   your mask of ashy fear and look—
>   look up, heart, to join
>   the cosmic dance.

This universe simply *is*. Every bit of energy, all that has being, is *Goddess*—infinite, timeless, eternal, whole and complete—knowing experience, knowing the particular, knowing time, knowing change, knowing other. The universe—all of this infinitely unimaginable energy—is alive, is conscious, is *love*.

The Creator of the universe permeates all that She creates. So consciousness has *us*, *we* don't have *it*. This turns the whole thing inside out. We are not *in* the universe, like water in a cup; we are not separate. We are part of the Goddess in the way atoms, particles, and molecules are part of the cells of the living beings they constitute.

Of course we are all one. We've known it for centuries.

It was 1624 when the poet wrote:

> No man is an *Iland*, intire of it selfe; every man is a peece of the *Continent*, a part of the *maine*; if a Clod bee washed away by the *Sea*, *Europe* is the lesse, as well as if a *Promontorie* were, as well as if a *Manor* of thy *friends* or of *thine owne* were; any mans *death* diminishes *me*, because I am involved in *Mankinde*; And therefore never send to know for whom the *bell* tolls; It tolls for *thee*.

Yet we experience change as other, as separate; we name things, objectifying them; we experience time, imagining a past and a future, a beginning and a death. We even objectify the Goddess, supposing Her elsewhere, to have abandoned us to bitter cosmic loneliness.

At the crossroads of time and eternity, of despair and love, hurtling toward the ultimate supreme consciousness, I begin to understand and embrace this paradoxical mixture of raw individuality with cosmic interbeing. This understanding permeates my being. It rides with me throughout the day. It's there as I sing the sun down every evening. It's there when I'm with friends while we talk about ordinary things, simply enjoying each other's company.

Wisdom is an intense vibration between: passion, intuition, creativity, possibility; and logic, elegant simplicity, the known, the remembered. My intuition must validate what I think; my mind must accept what spirit knows; spirit must allow temperance.

As a thinker, I want to know everything; as a contemplative, I dwell in the cloud of unknowing, where everything is nothing. But *nothing* is ... *everything*.

So here we are, consciousness made manifest as incarnate—embodied spirit—and needing dinner. Always, there is this question of how we are to live. Babies need to be rocked, the dying comforted. We may *not* suppose it is only spirit that matters.

There is a Zen saying, "Enlightenment begins with doing the dishes."

It's easy to love the Goddess of the Rainy Country. Her archaic beauty gentles the soul into a soft timelessness. She caresses you with the intimacy of near-rain—never quite falling, droplets settling everywhere, dazzling hair and face. You can hear the faint trace of Her cosmic laughter as pure, fresh water rushes off the mountains into the great river, as the skeins of fog dance and weave at the edge of invisibility in the high forest.

When I lived in Arcata, I often drove south along the coast, through those venerable forests. Everywhere, the green presence of trees, the redwoods; so tall, so many, those magnificent trees. And so ancient. Such a great crowd of them, looming, accompanying me for miles along that lonely road. I would drift into a dream state. Stopping at one of the groves, I would walk a little, savoring the springy, pungent forest floor. Then, after pressing my face into the rough, gritty bark for a moment, look up. And up—into the tallest living beings on earth.

The silence is stark.

We try to own these trees. We name them, call them sentinels, icons, we speak of serried ranks, of majesty, as though they were like us. They aren't. They are beings of a different order, alien to us. We can't begin to imagine what sort of deep consciousness they hold in their core. They don't have central nervous systems like us—they are plants. They communicate through their intermeshed roots, create environments we call forests. They are great vortices of highly organized energy. So powerful. They endure.

Not so easy, the Goddess of the Asphalt. Loving Her takes practice; it is an acquired joy. All that time when I was studying systems design and then working for Southern Pacific, I would go from my cottage in Kensington into the heart of San Francisco—underground beneath the bay by train or following the concrete multilane highway across the bridge by bus—into the stone world of the financial district.

At first, I sought out the oases. After covering over the living earth with asphalt and concrete, people put out trees in tubs and dotted their neighborhoods with little green parks or made little gardens on the rooftops. And there were armloads of flowers for sale on nearly every street corner. Every day at lunch time I would explore, looking for bits of life on favorite streets or down by the waterfront, sometimes bringing back flowers for my desk to defy the bleak flatness of computers, cubicles, and fluorescent lights.

I found I preferred the bus to traveling underground because the highway followed the shore of the bay, built on filled-in wetlands. There was a large black snag jutting up near the highway just before the Berkeley city limits, and most mornings a great sleepy owl perched there after her night's hunt in the marsh, oblivious to the city.

I tried to transform my judgment of what seemed ugly and learn what in its essence was beautiful in some way. When I stepped off the bus into the rushing storm of diesel fumes, it was like battling an arctic blizzard, the aroma was that strong. I would close my eyes for a moment and will myself to remember the pungent forest, visualizing a walk in Muir Woods, soft needles underfoot instead of concrete, perhaps a faint breeze, shriek of eagle replacing scream of brakes. Some days it seemed as though I was truly there.

Well, almost. But I did emerge from that awful diesel barn with the hint of a smile, my head high. I knew the earth was still there, deep below the buildings. Even the cement and tar had, after all, come from the earth, were a form of it. Instead of relegating asphalt and all that it stands for to ugliness, I began to see how it, too, is sacred, how it fits with everything else.

I looked deeper. Isn't *everything* from the earth? Why, just because the natural world is not shaped by humans, should we suppose it to be sacred, while saying the artifacts of humankind are not? Are we not also sacred? Are not our works?

Then I realized how this place is filled with lots and lots of people; after all, that is what a city is all about. They are busy, noisy, hardly perfect, surviving, loving each other (or not), seeking their places in the world. In a high window, I see someone rocking a child to sleep; in another, someone is laughing, cooking a meal for a friend, lighting candles, pouring wine; in another, an old woman sits quietly alone, reading a book. These are the redwoods of the Asphalt Country.

The Asphalt Goddess is a working goddess, up to Her elbows in dishwater and computers. She's a little sunburned and untidy and not at all serene. There is much that is lost or broken here for Her to heal. Her justice is mercy. Her compassion falls everywhere, soft and hot.

A flat, dull sea after all those storms.

A rain you cannot see but everything
is wet.

Lighthouse still flashing, even though
it's well past sunrise.

A day of grace—somber—for
loving, remembering.

I am an ordinary woman, whispering.

Remember. Remember who you are.

THEN

The aborigine tells her story, all the while drawing
in the sand with her *mirlbindee*, her stick.

She says they go walkabout. They clean up the
waterholes so the earth can breathe.

The animals, the birds, the creeks—they are
all speaking.

The kangaroo breathes out the first breath.

She says her father was a magic man, that he
carried meteorite stones that had special sacred
powers because they came from the universe.

Her mother often sat for hours under a tree.
Every day she woke up before dawn to dance
and sing the Sun up.

She tells the story of the Seven Sisters, which
teaches us about passion and desire and the
fruitfulness of the earth.

She does not mention the kangaroo again,
nor walkabout.

I am old. I am like a tree that knows nothing but wind. All my life I have lived within a shroud of protection in order to survive in a culture that hated me and did its best to kill me, to break me into pieces, to cut off the sweet fresh air.

No one knows what a woman could be were she to grow up safe in a world of love and respect. Oh, what might I have been?

Deeply alienated, I live in a country of dysfunctional and desperate immigrants. I have no tribe, no people, save my immediate family. Small wonder that I love this island, this *place* I have known all my life, so profoundly.

I am well aware that the indigenous people were uprooted, losing their homes, so that I, roots lost, can make mine here.

I gingerly offer the reparation of a shared love.

Memory is a strange land.

I'm not always certain of the facts, which year it was, or where, but I remember the emotions clearly—my mother's anger when another little boy broke my brother's glasses on the cement floor of the garage, my father's sadness when he didn't know if he wanted to care for the roses after my mother died.

Even this morning, I watched three loons fishing in the bright, calm sea—but perhaps they were grebes.

Yet I remember the wild joy I felt when I watched the ospreys come back after last winter. Or perhaps it was two winters ago.

Since forever, there have been eagles nesting in the highest fir on the hilltop behind the cabin. And there were people here, living gently in the thick forests, their long canoes moving swiftly among the dark islands, the spawning salmon choking the rushing creeks.

Before the counting and weighing and selling began, the Indians honored the salmon and the eagle and the fat marsh ducks. And they loved the cedar trees; they would sing a song to the tree before stripping its bark or cutting its wood.

It is a small thing, but when we catch a fish to eat, we remember them and return the uneaten parts of the fish to the sea just as they did.

My father's father was one of the first white men to buy land here. I like to think that he watched one of the great-grandfathers of the eagle I watch today.

There was an old Snohomish settlement at the head of Cultus Bay, a mile or so south of here. On the way to the clam beds, the berry patches, the racks of smoked salmon, surely someone rested here on this sandy beach, sheltered under the maples, drank the sweet spring water. I feel as close to them as I do my ancestors in Norway, as bonded by place as I am by blood.

The native people's oral history is so much richer than mine—grandmothers remembering grandmothers remembering grandmothers ... I can't remember either of my grandmothers ever mentioning their grandmothers. My elders are lost in mist on another continent, their stories meager and wildly romanticized.

Yet someone raised those resolute, lonely women. Shadow figures, teaching their girls how to cook and sew and how to braid their hair. And especially how duty comes before everything. There must have been songs and stories and laughter along with all that relentless hard work, but they are lost now.

I know some things. I can see in my mirror the high brow and wide blue eyes of the Norwegian women. I share my grandmothers' intelligence, their seriousness, that patient perfectionist's attention to every detail, their courage and tenacity facing down life, their quiet stubbornness.

I have not known who came before my grandmothers and their shadowy parents. But my youngest daughter, Sarah, has been indefatigable in chasing down old names, looking at census listings and obituaries, visiting the old towns, perusing historical accounts. She is a journalist and knows how to find out what she wants to know, and she found my grandmothers' people!

I am bemused to know these things now, like fossilized footprints hinting at some long-gone journey, this obscure part of me turned up to the light. Yet I feel richer, more anchored, somehow, knowing about the farm, Åas, northwest of Oslo, where my grandmother—my mother's mother—was born, and that Sarah has gone there, talked to cousins. It's almost a remembrance, with people to love.

And more: Ann Foster, the ancestor of my other grandmother—my father's mother—accused of witchcraft in Salem all those centuries ago. Her young daughters, wild with Salem's strange hysteria, were thought to be bewitched by her. Ann said she must be a witch if the elders said so. I imagine her, like her descendants, stoic and dutiful. Was she bewildered? Terrified? Or resigned, obediently believing her Puritan ministers that she was already damned? She died in prison before she could be tried. I am filled with a poignant welling up of love and compassion that I pour back down the years for this almost-remembered grandmother.

A hundred logs came floating by
to pay an early morning visit,
but then the tide changed
and they all went home again
without saying anything.

I was a little girl, just five, when I first came here to the island in the summer of 1932. My brother, Kenny, was about to turn nine. First-growth timber was a thing of the past, all logged out. The euphoria of those early days had vanished in the face of the Great War, the influenza epidemic, and now, the Depression. Maxwelton was barely a village—a string of houses facing a narrow beach. At the end of the road, the General Store sagged, derelict, next to the gapped-tooth rotting pilings of the old pier.

After that the beach was isolated and lonely, with no road and few buildings. My dad made a little path with a plank across the creek so that we didn't have to trudge through the heavy sand and the immense piles of driftwood that accumulated from all that logging. It wound past a tiny, seldom-used cabin built down in a small clearing way out in the driftwood, then past even tinier twin cabins, hiked up on stilts in the creek's marsh. Crammed onto the narrowest, most useless, least expensive chunk of beach property available, these cabins stood empty, except for the two weeks of vacation time annually allotted to the two postal workers who owned them.

Then a little further down the dwindling trail there were the rotting remains of my grandfather's buildings that had by then collapsed in the relentless rain. There was still a functioning outhouse and a sturdy boathouse built part way into the hill. We swept it out, patched up the roof and there was our summer home—one long room flanked by two empty windows with prop-up shutters, a thick plank floor, and a door at the west end. We called it simply *Camp*.

Beyond our place, there were two crude, narrow unpainted shelters, abandoned. Then, surprisingly, a cottage, rather elegant by beach standards, with its huge fireplace, two west-facing glass windows, and a partition at the rear forming a tiny bedroom and a tinier kitchen. It was furnished with a stout table and it even had shelves. Astonishingly, at Maple Point, after a mile or so of cliffs with their shifting rock fall, there was an improbably elegant and well-kept two-story house, gleaming white, with proper windows, a porch, and a commanding view of the whole Sound.

My dad, who already loved this place—he'd spent his teen summers here—quickly built a shelf for the water buckets, a rough table with benches to go out front, and a short plank walkway to the beach. But my mom had grown up in Montana and didn't know what to do. After she got in a fine black wood stove, cots to sleep on, a lantern, water buckets with a dipper, a quilt to hang crosswise for a little privacy, orange crates for dishes and other treasures, and elegant mosquito net curtains for those blank windows, she stayed in the dark boathouse with my brother and me, feeling lonely. One day my dad took her by the hand and said, "Come on, we're spending the day outside." Kenny and I trailed along and soon we were exploring the world of squishy, scritchy critters and slippery seaweed and barnacles and sand that squirted at you.

The summer I was six my dad built the cabin. I marvel now at how he got all the materials there. From the end of Maxwelton Road it was hump it all down the beach—mattresses, cots, lanterns, buckets and pots, coils of rope, the axe, the crosscut saw, the shovel, the froe, the peevee, all our clothes, sacks of rice, beans, oatmeal and other groceries, a few precious books, and a chess set.

"What is a froe? A peevee?" Kater, my oldest daughter asks, eighty-five years later.

The froe was used to split shakes. It was L-shaped, with a strong wooden handle and a thick, adjustable blade set at a right angle. Take a large block of cedar or other straight-grained wood, set it up with the grain vertical, place the blade carefully for width and slant, then, handle in one hand, hammer in the other, slam the blade down the grain to get one shingle—just like slicing cheese. It's surprisingly easy if the blade's sharp. Does anyone split shakes by hand anymore?

The peevee (or peavey) is a long, strong pike with a sharp metal point and one curved, hinged, sharpened tine near the end, resembling an elongated h. It is used for stabbing, grabbing, and rolling logs.

The froe, the peavey, and the crosscut saw all still reside in the back workroom of the cabin.

Getting the lumber there for the cabin was fun. Why haul something that floats? My dad built a splendid raft out of all the lumber that had been delivered at the end of the road: two-by-fours, two-by-sixes, tongue-and-groove shiplap. Window frames, rolls of black tar paper for the roof, boxes of nails, hinges for the door, chimney blocks, and the little truncated pyramids of cement that were to be our foundation posts all sat on top.

There it is, held forever in my young memory: Daddy, his pants rolled way up, long pole in hand, edging this awesome contraption slowly southward on the gently heaving incoming tide. Kenny and me running alongside on the beach, jumping and shouting encouragement.

Taken from the pages of *Popular Mechanics*, the plan was simple enough. Designed to keep sawing to a minimum, the cabin was twenty-four-feet long, the length of the lumber, with one end partitioned off to make a dinky bedroom, with room for a set of bunks, and a dinkier kitchen, complete with stove and one long counter for the water buckets. It had windows on either side of a sturdy front door, with a porch across the front.

After the ground was smoothed and leveled, the foundation stones set, the beams leveled, my dad got a young man from the village to help with the framing—everything squared off and true vertical. Soon we had shelter of sorts. Then, long hours finishing the roof, nailing on the siding, putting in the floor, adjusting the sliding windows. Inside there were bare rafters and raw studs—no insulation, no interior siding, no ceiling, and of course, no wiring, no plumbing. Mom thought it should blend in with the surroundings, so it was painted a soft driftwood gray with bark-brown trim.

Soon the cabin was almost finished—it was time for a party! Kenny and I, put to bed early to make room for the guests, peered out through the slots of the bunk at all the giant grown-ups talking and laughing, free of care for a magic, festive moment. To mark the occasion, my dad wrote their names on the front door, starting a tradition that has covered the door with the signatures of guests down the years. At the center you can still read those first names, printed in my father's precise engineer's hand under the legend "Housewarming, August 28, 1933."

A few years later, my dad added on a kitchen wing and a workroom, expanding the old kitchen into the front bedroom; we didn't have to eat or sleep in the main room anymore. And we had a coldbox—three plain boards with a screen—on the shady back porch, plus a large bucket filled with chilly spring water for keeping milk and cheese fresh; it was almost as good as our icebox in town.

Wintertime break-ins were a problem with so remote a cabin, so we had strong shutters fitted to each window, with long bolts going through holes in the window sash, washers and nuts worked on from the interior. It was a heavy job lifting these shutters in place. We had our lesson on orderliness: a nail above each bolt for storing the washer and nut, and the wrench always but always kept on the little shelf next to the front door so we could find it easily when we first arrived at the dark cabin each summer.

Yet, despite all that, we'd leave the smallest shutter, on the bunk-bedroom window, a trifle ajar, in case of fishermen caught in a storm, looking for shelter. This was a common enough occurrence. We would leave the kerosene lamp with matches and a can of beans out on the counter; when we arrived the next summer, the beans would be gone, replaced by a scrap of paper with "Thanks" written on it. No one ever damaged anything or disturbed our secret compartment—a sliding board under the shelf by the front door with room for a few small tools and some kitchenware.

Camp has always been the heart of family to me. I grew up here, remembering, dreaming, worshiping, loving. Now my children bring their children here.

It is where Kenny and I learned about the tides and the stars and the way eagles fly. We had fires on the beach at night while watching the stars come out, or we would huddle close inside when there was fog or mist.

We learned how to swim, how to row a boat, how to build a fire. We learned to play safely, to avoid stinging nettles, to keep clear of deep water and crumbling sand cliffs and unstable piles of logs. We learned to fish and dig for clams and where to gather the best blackberries.

Kenny built marvelous rafts, choosing well-balanced logs which we would float home at hide tide, nailing the planking at an angle to hold against the waves. For its anchor we would bury a box of stones deep enough to hold all summer, careful to have its rope long enough to reach the surface at high tide.

Electric lines and sewer connections weren't considerations back then when building on hard-to-reach sites. Everyone had outhouses tucked back among the bushes, sometimes softened by ivy or other vines. Water came from wells or springs. At first, we hauled our water from the town well in Maxwelton. Later, my dad developed a spring on the hill which kept our personal water barrel well-filled. There was plenty of driftwood for heating and cooking, and kerosene lamps, candles, and flashlights for nighttime light.

All the tools were human-powered. Sometimes a particularly fine log would drift in for the makings of many good fires, and my parents would set up sawhorses on the beach and go at it, each at one end of the crosscut saw, counting softly back and forth to keep the slow rhythm steady.

After a storm, we would all go out to scavenge the beach, hunting whatever flotsam the tide had brought in: pretty bottles, lumber, glass floats all the way from Japan, netting, an oar, once a large round wooden spool for wire that made a fine table.

One time my dad found a gnarled chunk of driftwood that greatly resembled the head of a horse. He fitted this to another slightly swaybacked piece to make the most splendid wooden horse a girl could dream of; he set it just south of the cabin, facing the sea and the mountains, forever riding into the sunset.

It is raining again.

It has been raining for weeks;
the sea is in a grand turmoil.

It is winter and I am by the sea.

My father's father, Robert Edouard Moritz, bought the two lots on the section line at the southern edge of Maxwelton not long after it was platted in 1905. He was hoping to join what had been planned as an intellectual and artistic community, with campgrounds and an amphitheater big enough to lure that traveling cultural show, the Chautauqua. He had just become the head of the University of Washington's newly formed Department of Mathematics and Natural Philosophy (what science was called then) after getting his doctorate from the University of Strasbourg, in Germany. Did he know how lonely it would be, after Strasbourg, with its learned professors, its great libraries and museums, to be an intellectual pioneer?

Once the land was his, he got to work making trails up the hill, developing a spring, clearing the upper meadow, digging the outhouse. He sawed logs to build a deep protective bulkhead. He planted fruit trees—apple, plum, cherry—bringing for decades to come a delightful blaze of spring blossom on the fir-dark hill and fruit for us summertime campers. He trudged up and down the trails trundling his wheelbarrow full of dirt—rich, loamy stuff—to build up the sandy topsoil, raising the land a few more inches above sea level. Unusually high tides do still sometimes flood the land.

My grandfather's buildings, which I know from a photograph, were a cluster of small shelters with shining windows and tent-like canvas roofs surrounding a deck, with a plank to the beach. There are two young women in the photograph, Mercedes, my not-yet-mother, and Florence, her younger sister. This would have been taken just before everything changed during the Great War.

Even with all this rich activity, he found time to write math textbooks, establishing the tradition for intellectual refuge here at Camp. Years later, my son Tom would come here, arriving one fall with about sixty pounds of books, in order to study Einstein's theories for himself. Magnificently thorough in his thinking, Tom had found his college professors' explanations incomplete and inadequate.

My grandfather dominated this family: With his blazing intellect and powerful will, he was unstoppable. My mother always gave him the profoundest respect; I think she was a little afraid of him.

He and I loved each other in a simple, direct way. He respected me; he *saw* me; his face always lit up for me. I never got criticized or told what to do; I felt free.

Sometimes he would set me a puzzle, eyes twinkling as I worked out the answer. Once he gave me a shiny 50-cent piece for working out that if you started at the equator and proceeded northwest, you would eventually end up at the North Pole. When he told me about Zeno's paradox, I told him Zeno was silly, asking the wrong question—of course we get where we're going.

He was my lifeline to worlds beyond imagination—worlds of ideas, and far worlds that were so different from the one I lived in. Before growing up on the farm in Nebraska, he'd been born in Germany and frequently returned there. He and my grandmother went to the Orient several times and once around the world. They were captured by a National Geographic photographer in 1935 setting out in a small boat to travel up the dangerous Yangtze River.

They always brought back exotic gifts. From China, an elegant cloisonné vase with intricately inlaid deep-blue enamel, and an urn with a fierce, painted dragon twining around it. From Japan, a miniature lacquered cabinet with little drawers and two doors that opened with a tiny key. There were Hansel and Gretel dolls for me: Hansel wearing lederhosen and a smart little feather in his green felt cap; Gretel, a little white apron with red cross-stitch and red ribbons in her pretty blonde braids. Once while on one of his walking tours, my grandfather carried a large cuckoo clock for his daughter-in-law (my mother) over the Alps from Germany into Italy.

Besides his beloved German philosophers, my grandfather was interested in Eastern ideas. Once I found, among some of the books left at Camp, a leaflet that described the many marvels and oddities of yoga. There were lurid, brightly colored drawings of peculiar beings, gaunt, angular, attenuated. Some of them had extravagant, gilt headdresses. Some of them had too many arms and legs. Their extremely uncomfortable-looking contortions were said to beneficial to one's health and well-being. I found this hard to believe—none of them looked especially happy.

I learned that *yoga* was the art that the *yogi* practiced. And I learned that people we thought were primitive and unenlightened thought that we in the West were the unenlightened ones. Interesting.

Grandpa died when I was twelve, before I'd come to understand what he saw—the cosmic beauty of mathematics, not just the wondrous puzzle of it.

I think a lot about him, how he lived and dreamed. When he played chess, he would take his queen off the board to give a good game, and I rather think he did *life* that way, evening the field in order to have friends. Who on earth was there he could talk to, think with? Was he always alone in his mind, immersed in philosophy books? Is this the lot of the intellectual pioneer?

Oh Goddess, I want to live forever, there's so much to think about. I know I am as brilliant as he was, yet not as steady, not as focused— culturally annihilated, adolescent thrust shattered into rubble. I was trying to be *acceptable*, when I should have been looking, knowing. Women don't get to grow up fierce and whole. Yet, because of this, I have a greater field of vision, undreamed of peripheral glimpses— ever shifting, subtly changing.

My mother always spoke of her father, John Kronschnable, in romantic terms: handsome strong, dark-haired, adventurous, the kind of man who made and lost fortunes. He went to the Klondike hunting for gold, but I never heard about any fortune, although his gifts were certainly generous—that stunningly beautiful kidskin doll, the pretty Haviland china, the rosewood piano. They were living in Butte, that bustling, desolate Montana mining town, when John died. He had contracted pneumonia after competing in a grueling rowing race, and never recovered.

On a bright morning after first snow,
I am thinking of my grandmothers.

Remembering ... remembering ...

My father's mother, Cassia Kennedy, was a quiet, stoic woman—patient, methodical—and so pretty. A high school teacher, she was a good partner for my ambitious grandfather and as frugal and oatmeal-loving as he.

She did everything his way, ordering their house according to his taste: his books, his prints, his leather couch, his rigorous schedule, the careful use of everything in the kitchen—count the eggs, measure everything, turn down the tiny blue gas flame. A careful and meticulous woman, this suited her. She kept her house clean, orderly. Her knives were sharp, the silver polished.

One night, in the apartment where she and my grandfather were living now that the boys were raised, Grandma thought she was stepping into the bathroom, and instead stepped into air and plunged down the long staircase to the front door. She broke her hip. The break never healed properly and she wasn't expected to walk again, but she did. After crutches, then canes, she somehow built up cartilage and muscle until she could take her daily walk with just one cane. My mother, with considerable awe, said she never complained. That was how I learned the word *stoic*.

After her fall, she and my grandfather went to live in the house on 34th Avenue NE, up on the hill behind the Catholic cemetery. Not too big, and all on one floor, except for the attic and basement. The main part of the house had a living room all across the front, a dining room, a huge gloomy kitchen, and two roomy bedrooms in the back.

It was a serious, spare house, but everything was of the finest quality—polished floors, with beautiful Oriental rugs, a magnificent oak roll-top desk (out of bounds to children), a narrow black leather couch, a slim mahogany rocker; and to remind them of their travels, etchings of Reims Cathedral and of Nike, the Winged Goddess of Victory.

Grandma had just one best dress in her closet, of the heaviest silk, elegantly designed, and just one ring—besides her wedding rings—of exquisite jade. She kept a sugar bowl made of silver, well-used and somewhat battered, on the round kitchen table, next to her quite ordinary little blue-and-white Chinese rice bowls.

I liked the contrast of this orderly place with my parents' home, which was full of clutter, something of a work in progress: sewing, painting, cooking, canning, gardening books, music, and newspapers strewn about—always something to clean up or put away. And I liked the contrast with the simple austerity of the cabin here on the island, where quality furniture was a sturdy orange crate, a bed crafted of driftwood, two water buckets, and a cast-iron stove.

Grandma was always gently kind to me, if austere, and treated me with great dignity. She never criticized me or expected me to be some different way. This made me feel grown up. I liked feeling respected.

She taught me a game called *Sixty-six*, a German game using a deck of twenty-four cards, the same as half a pinochle deck. There were no chips; you had to remember everything—all the melds and what cards were played. This was a delightful challenge. I looked forward to our games eagerly.

After Grandpa died, Grandma moved to an apartment in the University District where she could easily greet her friends as she carefully walked with her cane up and down University Way every morning, checking in with her friend at the China Shop, then on to the bookstore, Bartell Drugs, and ending up at Manning's Cafeteria for a hot lunch.

I never knew her dreams, only her duty.

I remember my mother's mother, Anna Christine Nelson, *here*, walking on *this* beach, picking berries, or sunning herself with her ugly tan stockings exquisitely rolled down into little hoops. She was alone then, poor and careful, spending endless time over the berries, bits of lace, patches, putting walnuts on the crisp icing of the only kind of cake she ever made.

I don't know much about Grandma's life. There is a photo of the homestead, a plain, weathered structure with a deep porch occupying one corner, and a steeply pitched roof making room for a sizable loft. It looks too small for a family of ten. It's about the same size as our cabin here at the beach.

Everything I know about the time before that was told to me by my deeply romantic mother. There's a strong streak of that running through this family—if you don't like your life, tell a different story. So family lore had invented a love story: An aristocrat is caught in a storm while sailing, shelters in a fjord with a family of prosperous farmers, falls in love with the daughter; they marry despite their parents' objections and flee to Minnesota.

All apparently fantasy born of those cold, lonely winter nights. There was no aristocrat, no yacht, no escape in the dead of night. A page from the May 1, 1885 census shows my grandmother as twenty years old and born in Norway. Evidently there were three children born in Norway before the entire family left the farm. Grandma wanted so much to be an American, she seems to have changed things a little and forgotten how old she was. She was ashamed of being born in Norway. She never spoke of the old days, nor would she speak Norwegian. I had a friend who would speak Norwegian to her sometimes, delighting in making her blush, but I never knew what he whispered to her.

Grandma kept silent about other things too, things she didn't want to remember. It wasn't until her old age that she told my mother that John Kronschnable (my mother's father) wasn't her first husband. Some time after she had finished her apprenticeship as a seamstress, she had married a brakeman who worked for the Great Northern Railway. Five-and-a-half-months later he was killed in a coupling accident. And then, after she married John, her first baby, George (listed in the family Bible), died before his first birthday. He too joined her long silence.

Grandma was a good, plain cook, so she opened a boarding house and did her exquisite sewing and needlework in order to raise her children on her own. My mother, just six, had to take care of her younger sister Florence and baby brother John (Buddy). They were wild and hard to control. Florence looked angelic with her long blonde curls, so she got away with a lot and my mother usually took the blame.

Grandma was determined to get this ardent bookworm to college, but there weren't any in Butte, so she packed up and went West—to Seattle and the University of Washington. She managed to rent a house, get furniture, find boarders, and get my mom enrolled in the University with a job at the library's bindery. The big oak table she bought then is still a favorite place for doing homework, down four generations—our best heirloom.

Grandma had remarried a kind, unambitious man, Michael Nice, who had been one of her boarders. He hadn't wanted to move, but she left anyway, so eventually he came too. He died when I was five, so I don't remember much, just that he laughed a lot and that he loved me; that he liked to tease my grandmother by pulling away his cup when she poured his coffee to see if he could fool her (hardly ever); that he would then pour great looping streams of condensed milk dancing up and down into his coffee; and that he sometimes wore a brilliant red fez with a shiny gold tassel because he was something called a Shriner.

Oh, yes, and that he grew the most glorious sweet peas along the back fence next to Grandma's pink hollyhocks.

Awakened to sunlight streaming through my back window, gleaming mountains, and a clear sky except for a low bank of clouds over the out-of-sight mountains of Canada.

My parents, Harold and Mercedes, weren't homesteaders themselves, but they had the settler's belief that they were able to do whatever was necessary. My father could and did fix anything—the plumbing, the roof, the car, the furniture. He built our beach cabin almost single-handedly. My mother could make a delicious meal out of unpromising leftovers or a bucket of clams or a fresh-killed farmer's chicken that had to be plucked and cleaned. She could cut down old clothes, unravel and reknit a worn-at-the-elbows sweater, turn sun-faded drapes, rework worn carpets. Still, she had a way of making things pretty—a little smocking or embroidery on the dresses she made for me, ivy stenciled on the kitchen wall, flowers or leaves or wild grasses in a jar on the plank table at the cabin.

Many years later, when I went east to the music school at Yale, I met people who couldn't do any of these things, things I had always taken for granted. People who grew up in a city or who went to private schools or who had remote parents, people who had never been camping, or cooked a meal, people who hated walking, who had learned neither art nor music. They seemed ill-formed to me, too pale, too flimsy. I was lucky to have such a frontier mentality. I was self-reliant and I knew I could handle whatever life would offer.

They were a beautiful couple, tall, dark-haired, elegant. He, raven-haired, hazel-eyed; she with never-cut, shining chestnut hair and eyes of brilliant blue. Both quietly shy, honorable, loyal, kind, hardworking; both A students at the University, he in civil engineering, she in history. It's hard to place them in the jazz age. They seemed to have left all that wildness to their siblings.

When they were courting, they lived about eight long blocks apart, not a long walk at all for young people not accustomed to cars. My father would bring my mother huge fragrant bunches of flowers from his father's garden. She was in for a surprise, though, after they married, for my father didn't know one thing about gardening—she had thought her life would be an endless flower garden.

They graduated with honors in 1918, marrying four years later, after my father had gone to MIT for a graduate degree and my mother had started teaching. When they married, my mother had to stop teaching—married women weren't considered suitable mentors for the young.

My father was a professor's son and much was expected from him. He settled down to the life of a professor, I think more because his parents wanted it than out of personal ambition or desire. He was quiet, stoic, obedient, like his mother.

My mother, a shy and quiet child, was a reader. She read everything: the popular *Elsie Dinsmore* books, the *Hardy Boys*, *Ramona*, Sir Walter Scott's romantic novels. In those days, eighth grade was the end of schooling for most kids—after that they went into the mines or household service—but my mother went on to high school where her favorite subject was Latin. They didn't have textbooks that eased you into the subject, just straight into Caesar and Virgil: "For tomorrow, please memorize the first eight lines." Her destiny to become a schoolteacher was firmly sealed.

My mother worked closely with Quaker groups all her life, helping others, although she never became one. She had been raised Lutheran, my father, Presbyterian. They made a compromise by joining the Congregational Church, a plain, independent group, strong on freedom of conscience, strong on respect for all people—my parents' kind of place.

My father never talked about theology, but he was strongly of the opinion that no minister or priest had the right to tell a person what to think. My mother happily settled into teaching Sunday School, painting large poster board scenes to help us kids understand God's magnificence. I remember one of them showing how large the universe is, all golden with sun and stars, dotted with planets—Saturn with its rings, and tiny, tiny blue Earth.

My brother was born August 24, 1923 in Seattle: towheaded, blue-eyed, a little shy. My mother wanted to name him Raoul. Perhaps she envisioned a romantic, dashing adventurer, like Douglas Fairbanks in *The Thief of Bagdad,* or perhaps she wanted to make up for having been named Mercedes, a Spanish name that didn't go well with her German surname, Kronschnabel. But my father stood firm; my brother was given his father's name, Harold Kennedy Moritz, with a small change so he wouldn't be called Junior: Harold Kennett Moritz.

When I was born, my father was working as an engineer in Long Beach, California. I was due to be born in mid-June. My mother was expecting the long hard delivery she'd had with Kenny, so she didn't pay much attention to a few early contractions. Suddenly it was too late, we were dashing across town in an ambulance, sirens screaming, barely making it to the hospital where my amazed mother happily welcomed a small 5½ pound, perfectly formed, bald-headed, blue-eyed baby girl—*me*—on May 17, 1927.

Evidently my mother hadn't learned much about her husband the first time—she actually thought she could get away with naming me Gretchen-Elspeth. My father stood firm once again and I became Margaret Jean Moritz.

1927 was a hard year for my parents. A few months before I was born, my father had survived a near-fatal attack of peritonitis brought on by a ruptured appendix. Then, shortly after I was born, my mother became seriously ill with a thyroid disorder. Her mother came storming down from Seattle to take care of us while my mother had an operation. With my mom gone, I refused to eat and had to be force-fed. I don't remember any of this, yet I still feel like cleaning my plate will please someone.

The year ended on a high note. My father was hired as an instructor at the University of Washington to teach hydraulics. I think both my parents were glad to return home and live among their families in Seattle again.

Mom is singing in the kitchen; she is happy. We have rented a house in Laurelhurst, where many families from the university have made their homes. Our house, a trifle shabby, needing paint, is set high above a curve in Laurelhurst Drive under a family of tall, dark fir trees. Mom loves to go for walks, taking me along with her. We ramble down one side of Laurelhurst promontory and back up the other, admiring the beautiful gardens and trees, the views of the lake. While all the houses have large yards, the mansions at the point are spectacular, with gardener-kept grounds and immense emerald lawns sweeping down to the lake shore with perhaps a pier or a boathouse.

She made a lovely home here. After much deliberation about the color, she washed the walls with tinted calcimine—paint was too expensive—and made drapes, hunted down old furniture, planted the rockery with snow-on-the-mountain, and gotten her mother to braid a rug for the front hall.

Most of my memories start here. I remember a little from before, static, vague: Mom's face deeply filled with worry, a hovering, blurry moon seen through the bars of my two-year-old's crib (I had whooping cough); her fear when Kenny first went away to that far-off alien and magical place called First Grade; and the dreadful day Kenny's turtle escaped. Who knows what turtle dream it was chasing—it climbed up a wall and, like Humpty Dumpty, had a great fall, breaking its shell; we all cried.

This house is fun for kids. It has two round-and-rounds. Kenny and I run shrieking through the kitchen, around the breakfast nook, across the living room, around the corner into the front hall, tear down the long narrow back hall to the pantry and back through the kitchen again. Good rainy day fun!

The upstairs is a different matter—too scary. We creep across the hall from our bedroom, through our parents' room, slowly opening the low door into a lightless storage room where the eaves slope down menacingly, the gloom casting an aura of weirdness over the trunks and heaps of boxes, the spider webs, the headless dress form, the crazy-tilted broken rocking chair—tiptoe, tiptoe. Then silently feeling for the latch of the far door, streaking back down the hall to the safe haven of our beds, where we break into relieved laughter.

But the place I love the most is back downstairs under the mantel in the space between the fireplace and the stairwell. It is just the right size for a playhouse, with its own tiny door. I have my dolls and books here; I am just learning to read. One of my favorite toys is a block puzzle—sixteen cubes faced with bright illustrations of fairytales. I love the way you could turn the cubes to get a new picture, with sometimes hilarious results: Little Red Riding Hood with the Three Little Pigs!

I earned this puzzle at the cost of a hard lesson. Mom decided to reward my good behavior and put up a chart ruled off into squares. I have to make my bed, set the table, and I can't remember what else, in order to get gold stars. Day after day after day. I hate it.

Oh Mom, I would do these things anyway, I want to learn how to do things right, how to grow up. You don't have to bribe me, measure my goodness.

I imagine crumpling up the chart, crunching up the stars. But I never do. I badly want that pretty puzzle my mother set as my reward. I should walk away from it, but I don't. I am only five, yet I know what I am doing working for those loathsome stars, every day losing a little bit of what I am too young to name: my integrity.

And all those times she'd chant that awful nursery rhyme at me while I'm sitting there on my little stool: *There was a little girl who had a little curl right in the middle of her forehead. When she was good, she was very good indeed, but when she was bad she was horrid.* I'm trapped, miserable. I just want to run away. I'm not rebellious or obstreperous, I just don't want to be flattened, I don't want to be kept in a box.

Oh Mom, what savagery do you imagine me capable of?

One afternoon, one of Mom's friends comes over. She is a large woman, respectable, wearing a dark dress, heavy shoes, hair pulled tight—a good woman. I am sitting on the floor, playing; I feel safe as long as I stay quiet. She comments on my prettiness, my goodness. She does not see *me*. I want to kick her in the shins, wake her up, tell her who I really am, that she would be amazed if she knew me. But I stay quiet. You want a good girl, Mom. But I am *not* a good, pretty little girl—how tiresome—I am *me*.

Twice, just this week, I've seen a seal.
It is the first time all year.

Its head is like a blob of seaweed or a
small buoy, but is clearly distinguished
by its delicate streaming wake, then its
sudden disappearance.

There were so many of them
when I was a child.

In the spring, with its lengthening evenings, all the kids would pour into the empty street after supper to play baseball and other games. Laurelhurst was a lovely, quiet neighborhood, full of children, and since our street had almost no traffic, it was always the center for the neighborhood games.

The sidewalks were just right for hopscotch or skating. Our roller skates were shiny metal and could be adjusted to size, the front and back held in place with a wing nut; the toes had clamps where the edges of the soles of our leather shoes slid in, tightened with a key. I kept my key on a pretty ribbon around my neck so I wouldn't lose it.

The older girls would bring out their long, magical jump ropes and do intricate maneuvers, often with two ropes at once, everyone chanting rhythmically. Or they'd play jacks or marbles. At some point, one of the older girls would takes charge of the younger kids to play *Simon Says*, *Mother May I*, or *Statues*.

The most fun for me were the big group games, like *Kick-the-can*, where we'd scatter throughout the neighborhood, returning to safety one by one with triumphant shouts of "Oley Oley Olsen free." Best of all, I loved baseball. What a truly wonderful game, where the fortunes of a team can change with a single great play—exciting to play, exciting to watch.

There were no parents involved. I don't know how things get decided; it was a sort of spontaneous combustion. Someone would shout "You're it!" Or a bat and ball would appear and suddenly the game was on. Mom's presence was felt only as a disembodied voice, softly calling into the lingering twilight, "Kenny, Peggy, time to come in."

It was in Laurelhurst where I met Stan Pocock. He lived across the street from us and was Kenny's best friend. He grew up to become a world-renowned shell builder like his father, George Pocock. We sometimes visited his father's workshop where those long, sleek cedar racing craft were constructed, since it was next to my father's Hydraulics Laboratory on Portage Bay. I mostly remember the distinctive smell, a blend of cedar, sawdust, varnish, machine oil.

Some sixty years after I had left Laurelhurst, Stan and I met again here at the beach on Whidbey Island. Stan had bought a house and was delighted to find his childhood friends again two doors down at Camp. And then of course I in turn bought the house from him and his wife Sue seventeen years later; *this* house—*Maris Stella*—the house where I now live.

Later I learned that Stan had used the leftover cedar shells from his workshop for his remodel, adding a two-bedroom wing and cottage. Every night when I lie down for the night, I delight with wonder that I am sleeping, like a Viking explorer, under an overturned boat!

How our lives intertwine,
unexpectedly crossing
so many years later.

My father longed to have his own boat. This never worked out for him, but when we were still a young family, this dream seemed possible. Once, he at least got a taste of his dream. One of his friends had a small boat which he chartered out to my father for one glorious cruise in the San Juans. Her name was Scamper.

I guess it was a tight squeeze for grown-ups, but at age five I thought it was perfect. A fine deck at the back was our living room; I was safely tethered to the mast when I played there. My mom would sit against the rail watching the birds that followed in our wake; she would peel potatoes, tossing the parings over her shoulder into the water to the impatient gulls.

A few steps down was the galley. The kitchen, of course, but on a boat everything is magical and has to have its own special name. The narrow floor here lifts off to reveal the heart of the boat—the motor, which frequently needs some sort of adjustment. No cooking, no coffee while my dad has the floor up. Once, he emerged from this greasy work holding up a spoon that had somehow fallen in!

There were four bunks, which did double duty, too. The upper bunks were just right for two small children, and a table folded out so that the lower bunks were seats by day, my parents' beds by night.

Up the steps was the pilot's room, a serious place—no yelling or playing allowed. There was the great wheel, called the helm, and all sorts of navigation charts, tide tables, binoculars, a compass, lamps, a foghorn. My mom had to stand out on the deck when there was dense fog, unable to see anything but swirling white in all directions, blasting away with great honks to ward off collisions.

My dad kept a log in the cabin, too. I was disappointed to find out this didn't look anything like a log but was just a sort of book. Everything's different at sea!

Leaving Seattle, we traveled west through the locks and into the Sound. We often visited the locks for a Sunday outing, watching all the different boats line up, tossing ropes to the boatmen, shouting greetings, walking precariously along the tops of the gates when they were shut.

Now it was our turn, handing out papers, tossing up ropes to tie us in, waiting for the clang of the bell warning that the gates are about to change. Then the back gate slowly closing, keeping the high water out, the water in the lock dropping, dropping, past the green slime, past the depth numbers painted on the walls, until we come to rest way down in the dark lock. The lower gate slowly opening, the ropes untied, motors started, and we file out with the other boats into the waters of the Sound.

We headed up the inside passage east of Whidbey Island toward Deception Pass. Then a frightening day! A large gray vessel approached us, a powerful cutter, with U.S. COAST GUARD emblazoned on it. They requested to board. They looked at documents. They searched; all the scarier for their being so polite. Did they really think we looked like smugglers or bootleggers? Of course they found no contraband.

We had been waiting for slack water, when the treacherous currents of Deception Pass became quiet with the turn of the tide. The Coast Guard told us we should just follow them through, no need to wait, but the Scamper didn't have a powerful motor like theirs and what followed was a near disaster. We tossed and banged, swirled around in a circle, inched past the menacing rocks, my dad fighting for control, exhausted, as we reached the safety of the western waters. A lesson to remember: Don't give your trust to the experts, listen to what they have to say, but use your own judgment!

We finished the rest of our vacation more calmly, catching fish, exploring islands, getting stuck at low tide, visiting old friends, picking blackberries, making beach fires, watching sunsets.

No whitecaps, no sails;
thick sodden winter rain
sends home the eagle's
white flash.

One day something magical happened. It was time for me to start school. Back then, few kids went to kindergarten. Most people thought that little children belonged at home with their mothers, that they were too young to start their formal education. Nursery school? Playdates? Not in the '30s. So I felt quite grand, trudging along with the big kids down our winding street, then following an old dirt track, a spooky fir forest on one side, a great green field on the other, to our modern one-story red brick school.

Here was a wonderful place, full of bright, colorful pictures, toys, lots of little chairs, a huge blackboard with chalk, all sorts of projects, and, of course, books. Since I was already an avid reader, I was advanced to the second grade after a couple of weeks. Arithmetic quickly became my favorite subject. I liked to *know* things, I wanted to know everything. I had found my calling. I became a thinker. This was serious grown-up stuff, so I thought I should be called by my real name now—Margaret—instead of Peggy.

The track to school was often muddy and filled with large rain puddles. Once the whole path was like a lake and I was too little to get through. I'll never forget what happened next. An eighth-grade boy, Buzzy Weeks, seeing my predicament, lifted me up and set me gently on the far side of the impasse, patted me on the head, smiled at me, and jogged on down the trail. Later, he was among the first to be killed in the War, but this one small act of kindness reverberates down the years.

With soft blonde hair and innocent blue eyes, I was a pretty little girl. One rainy day later that year, I came to school in a black slicker and rain hat that had been my brother's but was way too large for me. My teacher thought the combination was adorable and had me go from room to room to be admired. I can't imagine that happening today. Those really were such innocent and naïve times.

When spring rolled around, I was chosen to be Queen of the May. What fun we all had, dancing and singing, weaving and reweaving the bright maypole ribbons.

The next year, at the end of third grade, this world ended. The owners of our house wanted it for themselves and we had to move. At the same time, my grandma (Anna) had been living alone for a couple of years and wanted to live in an apartment just off University Way, so my parents decided to buy her house on 19th Avenue NE, half a block north of the University campus.

I lost all my friends, my wonderful school, my favorite places to play, and all the secret nooks and crannies of that delightful house on Laurelhurst Drive.

Stunningly gorgeous morning!

Frost everywhere, mountains
richly covered in snow, with easy
light picking out the foothills in
that special way that happens
just after sunrise.

Porcelain blue sky, calm waters,
a waning gibbous moon about
to set.

The neighborhood of my new home took some getting used to—there weren't any kids! No more baseball in the street, no twilight games of *Kick-the-can*, no mothers' voices calling us home. On one side of us, the widow and her snarly dog; on the other, the Alpha Xi Delta sorority, with its sweeping lawn and lattice fence full of soft pink roses; across the street, a gleaming white fraternity house, with tall Greek columns defining its half-circle portico; and to the back, across the alley, an older nondescript house with three stories of open sleeping porches across the back, full of boisterous young men—a boardinghouse. Up and down the streets, more of the same.

Grandma's old home was a dark brown hulk, substantial, ugly, set high on the steep slope rising from 19th Avenue NE, a half block north of the University, its square plainness somewhat obscured by the solid upper balcony and the front porch, also solid, supported by several large, round pillars. No windows in view.

The front approach was relentless cement. True, two splendid locust trees grew in the parking strip, but then came sidewalk, high, rough retaining wall, steep, irregular cement steps up to two tall sentinel laurel bushes—dark, heavy, overgrown—and on to the cement pathway curving left around to the porch steps. Here, my grandma had tried to make things better by planting a hopeful blue hydrangea.

Inside, it was dark, too. Most of the north side was occupied by the staircases and the south was close to the widow's house, another ugly, dark brown hulk. Ours was a house for duty and frugality. My mother can't have been happy there, but she tried to make a good home out of it. Not much laughter. Both my parents were serious and shy. They needed a lighter house.

I didn't know any better and this was my childhood. When we moved again, I'd be thirteen. So I burrowed in, growing, playing, learning, dreaming. This was a good time for me and I was happy, doing things I loved, exploring everything, finding out about different worlds, different ways of thinking, making a rich, lifelong friendship. I felt entirely secure in who I was. I didn't know it could be any other way.

My room was high up in back, a narrow, glazed porch without heat, the windows on a long side, the bed just fitting at one narrow end, a bureau at the other. It had cold, smooth linoleum and wallpaper with little black and red Chinese designs, augmented by my doodling. To get to it, I had to go through the back bedroom where Doris, the university student who was my mom's helper, stayed; my closet was off her bedroom, the bathroom down the hall. My room was far away, safe, all my own.

I loved that gloomy old house.

A half block away was the University of Washington campus. This was before the great dormitories were built and before the 45th Street viaduct gave access down the cliff below 21st Avenue NE to the fill below. Most of the UW buildings were concentrated near the quad at NE 42nd Street and University Way, while the area near us on NE 45th Street was lightly wooded, with many paths leading into the main campus. University Way was only five blocks away, where there were shops, restaurants, movie houses, banks, soda fountains, and—oh, the joy of it—bookstores.

Just as these delights thinned out at NE 50th Street, there was a whole block enclosed by chain link fencing and covered with gravel. In the center sat another hulk of a building, this one gray: University Heights Grade School where I was about to start 4th Grade. This was plainly a serious place, nothing frivolous or decorative anywhere. There was a long set of stone steps up to the high first story with its heavily oiled wooden floors; then on up to the second floor with its library and upper grade classrooms.

My dad went to University Heights School, too! Back then there were dense woods north of the campus between his house on 21st Avenue NE and the school on NE 14th Street (now called University Way). I remember him telling me about having to skip school whenever a bear wandered into the area. I thought it would be wonderful to have a *bear* day! Much more glamorous than a snow day.

I was a big kid now, in the fourth grade. There was work to be done here. Not only was I known as a smart kid and a University kid, but since my father had gone to school here, intellectual obligation hung heftily on the name Moritz. An exhilarating challenge!

I tore through fourth grade by Christmas. All that was required of me was to read *Children Around the World* and memorize the second half of the multiplication table, the sixes through twelves. And so, when the new term began in January, I became a fifth-grader with a whole new class to fit in with. It was an unusual class full of bright, argumentative, determined, and eager kids: Bobby Benbow, Wing Luke, Margaret Fels, Jeremy Gilbert, and Julia Gay Ballantine. These were my new friends. Real peers. This was high fun!

Julia and I quickly became best friends. She was a tomboy, with a no-nonsense Dutch bob and an attitude to match, and, being stronger than I, much better at baseball. I was better at arguments and organization and attention to detail and more of a dreamer. We were about equally stubborn.

We were both University brats—Julia's father was a professor of mathematics in my grandfather Robert's department—so we understood each other quite well and were comfortable in each other's homes. Our mothers told us that we had already met at a faculty gathering when I was a baby, Julia nine months older, and how with great glee Julia had pronounced proudly, "Peggy wears diapers, Ju Ju wears *union suits.*" Baby bonding. That bond lasted a lifetime.

Julia and I want to know everything. We are figuring out how people think, how brains work. We talk, swinging on the big, green canvas front porch swing. We bike to school together, do our math homework together, play piano pieces for each other. We collect shiny horse chestnuts; we do jump rope marathons. We make maps, we take hikes. We make plays from the stories of music we've learned. We do everything together.

At Camp, we stay by ourselves in the "pest" house, reading by flashlight; we shiver by the bonfire after swimming in that cold salt sea; we roast marshmallows; we dig for clams. Sand everywhere with its different textures, muddy, oozing through our toes, or coarse and biting, too hot to walk on, or so spongy from shrimp or slimy with bright green seaweed we can hardly get across it. Minnows tickling toes. Mosquitoes whining as they zero in. Nettles' sharp sting.

We learn the tides, the weather, how to make a fire, how to use the wood stove. Best of all we watch the stars come out in that late northern twilight, or, waking in the night, we trek to the outhouse, awkward with sleep, and look up at the strange, unknown sky, everything shifted, a new configuration of starlight. Or watch the storms, rains pounding the little cabin, lightning dancing in the mountains sometimes; or watch the rare northern lights, eerie, green, half-imagined.

And the punctuations of manmade things: great cargo ships going out with the high tide, the light flashing every evening from Point No Point, or the Princess steaming past the Point in the morning, at precisely 10:24, on her way to Victoria. There is just time to slip into our still clammy bathing suits and get out to water's edge before her wake's great waves come pounding in—our morning's daily delight.

Julia and I explored everything. We biked all around the neighborhood streets: wide, chestnut-lined 17th Avenue NE with its center strip and its handsome houses, and the winding, steep Ravenna Boulevard where Julia lived. Or we'd explore what the parks that were behind Julia's house had to offer—woods in a steep ravine, a small clear stream, an alarming swaying suspension bridge. We would go up and down University Way, checking out the bookstore, the drugstore, and all the wonders of Woolworth's five and dime; we'd peer into the bank where our pennies were kept, check out the latest in pretty postage stamps (we were both avid collectors), sniff to our hearts' content the seductive aromas of Manning's cafeteria, or watch the latest invention: the big, bread-slicing machine at work at Van de Kamp's bakery.

Our last stop on University Way was our favorite, The Shop of China, where we'd finger the curios, and admire the dogs and dragons, the satins with their flashy colors, the brass and ivory and jade, and soak up the heavy scent of incense. *Everything* in that store was strange, suggesting worlds full of adventure across vast oceans, worlds we could scarcely imagine, so different from ours in every way. But we knew they existed, those other worlds; my grandparents had traveled there, and Mrs. Roberts, the store's patient owner, had lived there, in China, as a missionary.

Other times we biked all the way over to the library on 10th Avenue NE where we methodically read our way through the children's collection. We earned all the stars and stickers there were in the various reading programs offered, then got permission (a parent's consent was needed) to take books out of the grown-ups' collection. We'd spend hours poring over the dictionary, studying the origin of words or poring over the long shelf of encyclopedia volumes with their lavish illustrations—all knowledge squashed into four or five feet.

Our favorites were the Ransome books, *Swallows and Amazons* and the rest of the series. These are adventure stories about children who live on an island, much like Whidbey. They have lots of friends, they have sailboats, they have an old rambling house. And they have freedom, as their parents are conveniently elsewhere, traveling. These are

English kids, so they have a housekeeper, eat strange food (kippers), and call a flashlight an *electric torch*. How exotic to a ten-year-old.

Then there was the University campus, a huge, green territory, an adult world where we roamed almost invisibly. We poked our curious noses into every building there to find out what might be on display. We peered at old manuscripts, examined dead bugs, stared at strange paintings and even stranger sculptures, listened to singers attempting ever higher scales, checked out the model of the Grand Coulee dam at my dad's hydraulics lab, admired the sleek, cedar racing shells in Mr. Pocock's crew house, sat on the stone bench under the pink flowering dogwoods, and explored every cranny of the Natural History museum—its dead animals and smelly artifacts, tools, baskets, dioramas of Indian village life, ragged garments, the war canoe, the Egyptian mummy.

We always ended up at the Chimes Tower just before five o'clock, when George Bailey, lugging his black tool satchel, would come toiling up the hill and down the other side to the gray shingled tower just off 18th Avenue NE, tapping his blind man's cane to find the path in. He would unlock the door with a large key and let us all in to the dusty, shadowy room under the bells, take out his pocket watch, touch its raised Braille figures to check the time, and release the broad leather straps that held the bell levers tight. Arranged like a giant's piano keyboard, these stout levers were attached to the ropes that rang the bells. Mr. Bailey would pound each lever with all his strength to begin that glorious peal—thunderous to us right below the bells—that signaled all over the campus and surrounding neighborhood that five o'clock had arrived.

After about ten minutes of strenuous play, Mr. Bailey would gather up his tools and trudge back over the hill. It was time for Julia and me to head home to our piano practice and our chores and our dinners.

When Julia and I became Girl Scouts, we proudly acquired all sorts of skills. There were camping trips, where we learned how to make fires (and to put them out), how to cook over the campfires, how to make a safe, dry camp and keep it clean, and how to respect the wildlife. We learned how to use and care for any number of tools, how to give first aid, how to read maps, and how to follow a trail. We learned about weather and tides and birds and wildflowers. I took this pretty much for granted—I thought these were things anyone should know how to do.

Girl Scouts had no ranks higher than First Class, so I couldn't become an exalted Eagle Scout, the highest Boy Scout rank. Instead, I went in for merit badges, eventually earning twenty-four of them—eight rows three deep marching up my uniform's left sleeve. They were pretty little things, some were symbols—the red cross, the treble clef—others were tiny pictures—a black pot over bright red flames, two folk dancers, knitting needles stuck into balls of yarn, brightly colored spools of sewing thread, a tiny globe for international studies, the two masks of drama, a row of books, a writer's quill, a compass, a seahorse, the seven stars of the Big Dipper.

To earn the Star Finder badge, Julia and I took our sleeping bags out onto the beach one clear night and set an alarm clock to wake us up every hour, so we could watch the Big Dipper swing around in its circle and be sure the North Star stayed put. (It did!) We had to see these things for ourselves.

One time we went to the campus observatory to look at the moon through the telescope my grandfather had repaired when he first arrived at the university.

Another time, when we were learning about mapmaking, we cycled over to the Arboretum and proceeded to pace off the road there, which swings about in a great circle. We would sight a tree or fence or a sign, make a compass reading, and pace the distance, then another and another, zigzagging our way around the road. But there was simply too much room for error—we could not quite get the ends of our map to meet. Still, it was a good enough effort to earn our mapmaker badges. While we were there, we learned enough about trees to earn our Tree Finder badges, too.

I didn't know until a lot later how important those years with Julia were. I learned how to be close to a friend, of course, and I learned how to do things—exploring, biking, swimming, playing chess, arguing, fantasizing. This was a rich time, my mind open to every possibility. I was laying down the mental habits of a lifetime, to be both logical and creative, to be meticulous and thorough, to be ambitious and stubborn. When someone would ask me what I wanted to be when I grew up, expecting the usual answer of mommy or teacher, I would exuberantly reply, "I want to be an actress and a writer and a musician and an astronomer."

With Julia I had learned to want to be true to myself. We weren't really old enough to think of careers, we were only ten years old, twelve at the most. I guess, looking back, we wanted to be authentic. We didn't want to do what someone else thought we should do; we wanted to know who we were.

I love the precision of my new vocabulary.

Tsundoku: the piling up of great numbers of unread books (not applied to booksellers).

Pogonip: frozen fog (especially beautiful on stark bare trees).

Gray-green water with underlay of taupe, slightly shiny, with an approaching storm.

Is there a name for that?

To get my allowance I had to keep an expense ledger, writing down every penny in its *in* or *out* column and figuring the balance. My father was teaching me responsibility. I soon learned to budget my lunch milk costs, my bus tokens—large, light coins with a hole in the center, worth 2½ cents—and my weekly savings, which I paid out every Tuesday into the school's savings program. I chose my treats carefully, learning to save up for big items: a book, a flashlight. When I was ten, I patiently and proudly saved up money from my allowance to buy an alarm clock, a classic, round, wind-up clock with two bells on top. Now I could wake up at 6:00 and practice my flute before breakfast. I wanted to be self-reliant.

My dad never commented on what I bought, other than something mild like, "I see you're collecting stamps now," but he always looked over my listings carefully. When I got older, I was amazed to hear friends talk about things they wanted and therefore *had to have* or *deserved,* and would get these things by whining to their parents.

I think I was born meticulous. When I was five, my Grandpa Nice commented with amazement at the way I was cutting out my paper dolls, working oh so carefully around every ruffle or curl or finger. I was equally amazed back. How else would anyone want to do it?

I loved complicated projects. Once, when I was stuck in bed with a light case of mumps, I made a whole orchestra out of pipe cleaners, toothpicks, and thread. I especially enjoyed making the harp and the rather manic conductor.

When other kids were making simple Christmas ornaments out of red construction paper, I got involved with pentagons and five-sided cones and glued together a gorgeous twelve-sided dodecahedron star.

In high school, in the new house we'd just built, I spent hours with a single-edged razor blade cutting away the background white on six lovely Audubon bird prints—blue jays, mourning doves, goldfinches— and mounting them on the panels of my white closet doors. A pretty touch in a rather small room.

When I was ten, I was determined to do what no one had been able to do—make pi come out even. Oh, I would be famous! I devoted every spare moment for two weeks dividing and dividing, seven into twenty-two, checking my work carefully, but no matter how long I kept at it, those numbers just kept repeating. Finally, my teacher gently told me that there were mathematical concepts that were not whole numbers. Oh, the injustice! The world was plainly more complicated than I'd thought.

How quiet our houses were. How endless the hours. The sounds of voices came from living people—songs that were sung in church or around a campfire, or perhaps my mom singing as she lulled me to sleep. Sometimes my dad softly played his black wooden flute. My mom played splendid pieces on the piano nearly every day, pieces I would later learn were written by Chopin, Brahms, Debussy, Mozart, Beethoven.

On rainy days, I played with my dolls, or read and reread favorite books. I loved the Norwegian fairy tale, *East of the Sun and West of the Moon*, full of charming but peculiar pictures like the Pied Piper of Hamelin, in his swirling, tattered cloak and tall pointed hat; or the ancient man with his long, crooked nose in *Why the Sea is Salt*; or the darling little boy in the Sarah Cone Bryant books who could never get things right, who was named—what a joy to one just learning to read—Epaminondas. And of course, *Winnie-the-Pooh*. Delicious.

As Kenny and I got older, we played cards—casino and rummy. Kenny made model airplanes. I collected stamps. We played anagrams or Parcheesi—our favorite until that wildly popular new real estate game came out—Monopoly. Who can resist play money?

Every Friday after dinner we went to the Egyptian Theater where the format never varied: a newsreel, a cartoon, previews, the *B* movie, then the main feature. Afterward, we would stroll up and down University Way, window shopping, before heading back home.

Saturday nights were for grown-ups—dancing at the Trianon or playing bridge with friends. Sundays, after a mid-day dinner, we would pile into the car and go for a drive. Sometimes we would end up at the Chittenden shipping locks in Ballard, or maybe the Seattle Art Museum—my dad's favorite place. If we wanted a longer excursion, we'd take a picnic up to Granite Falls.

Summers at the beach were simple enough. Endless playing on the tide flats, swimming, rowing our little green boat, building catamarans and the raft, dreaming fantasy worlds out of the crazy-shaped driftwood, playing chess on rainy days. Sometimes, a party at Woodland

Hall, with square dancing; or ice cream cones when we went shopping in Langley; or a hike to Maple Point to get clams. Evenings, a beach fire, sunset, singing, and long, long moments waiting for the stars to come out.

To make up for those long twilit evenings, we always had a quiet time after lunch, when my mom read to us. Most of the great plays of Shakespeare, or Van Loon's *The Arts*, or H.G. Wells' *Outline of History*. She read Wells' description of eternity—how a huge mountain is slowly worn down by a small bird, who sharpens its beak on this rocky mass every hundred years; when it is worn away, one day of eternity will have passed.

This strong image was etched into my young mind. But it's not quite right—eternity isn't merely endless, it's a condition of there being no time at all; sort of like childhood.

Again a gentle, misty rain, with a dull,
chiffon sky, ivory light lifting from
Canada, the only horizon the
heavy sea's edge.

Now the strengthening wind begins to
stir up dancing whitecaps, the sea
darkens to a greenish bronze.

I am glad I have my fine black stove.

The strawberries were ripe so my grandma was making shortcake. In those days, nearly everything was made from scratch, so cooking took up most of the day. But that was changing. My grandmother remembered washboards and sadirons and root cellars and horses and a time before telephones. We had a washing machine with an attached handwringer, a plug-in electric iron; an oak ice chest; a car you cranked to get started. And a radio! We had a coal furnace, too, so we didn't have to chop wood. We sliced our own bread, although we usually bought it from the baker, and we ground the beef ourselves and sliced the bacon. Advertisements, with their brand names, were just beginning to change what people thought they needed: Kellogg's cornflakes, Franco-American spaghetti, Wrigley's chewing gum, Jell-O, Ipana toothpaste, Ivory soap, Kleenex, Kotex, Gillette razor blades; how archaic it all sounds now.

Keeping house, especially in that house, was hard work—endless chores and fixed schedules.

The first chore of the morning was my dad's, to go down in the dark depths of the basement and stoke the furnace and shovel the coal. The last chore at night was to bank the fire and close down the draft. During the day, my mom would have to shovel the coal every few hours. Later, we bought a hopper, an invention that fed the fire gradually throughout the day and had to be loaded only once a day. There was no thermostat. Hot air was forced through ducts into the registers of the various rooms of the house. If it got too warm, you closed the register. This seemed like a great improvement over the Laurelhurst house, with its single gas floor furnace in the front hall. The hard thing about coal was that it made everything dirty with greasy soot. My mom really tried, but no matter how often she scrubbed, the coal dust won.

Oatmeal was at 7:00 every morning. I had to be in from playing by a little past 5:00 p.m. to practice my piano lesson and then help with dinner. Bedtime was firm. My dad would become upset and restless if dinner wasn't ready at 6:00 or at least 6:15. Yet my dad found great pleasure in life's small moments, a good pun or bit of wit, a game of chess, a trip to the art museum, a bowl of cornflakes just before bedtime. Sometimes he'd play his black wooden flute or the only piece he'd ever learned for the piano: "Lola." My mom was serious, without a sense of humor, and often critical, so I was glad that he showed me how to have fun with little things.

All the interesting things happened at the back of the house, leaving the front to its gloomy dignity. Two slanted doors, locked with a large padlock, opened into the coal chute, where the coal was dumped with a roar straight down into the huge bin in the basement. There was an alley running between 18th and 19th Avenue NE, dusty or muddy depending on the season. Our garage sat at the edge of it. Electric and phone lines ran in from it. Garbage got collected out back and all the delivery trucks used this alley. Every morning, the milkman brought our bottles of milk and cream up to our back porch and every night we put the empties out for collection. The ice man came twice a week, with a big block of ice clutched in his tongs, to fill our perpetually needy icebox. Emptying the drip pan was another daily chore. The alley was also the way I went to and from school or to see my friends. We hardly ever used the front street.

The laundry lines were out back, too. Laundry took up a lot of my mom's time. We did have that child's delight: a laundry chute. What fun to toss your socks into that little doorway and have them tumble way, way down to the basement laundry basket.

After that, hard work for my mom. Fill the washing machine and shave the bar of Fels Naphtha soap into it; start with the white laundry. The machine sloshed everything back and forth with its oscillating paddles, but that's all it did. You had to time it, then feed the sheets through the wringer attached to the side of the machine into the cement sink filled with rinse water, slosh all this about with a stick or paddle, then through the wringer again into another sink for the second rinse, this one with bluing added to prevent an aged yellow tinge, more sloshing, and more wringing, ending finally in a laundry basket. Using the same water, now cooler, you'd repeat all of the above for the next batch of sheets, then white clothes, and again for the colored laundry. Finally, you'd let down the hose from the washing machine and send the water spewing into a drain in the cement floor.

After cleaning the soap scum from the washing machine and the cement sinks, you'd lug the baskets of heavy wet sheets and clothes up the stairs to the half-landing and out the side door and back to the yard with the waiting lines. You'd peg the clothes to the line with great care, to avoid dangling a sheet or shirtsleeve onto the ground. Hope for sun and a light wind! If it rained, you had to take everything down and hang it out on the lines strung across the basement ceiling.

One more bit. You had to take the shirts, aprons, dresses, and napkins, which you had saved out, up into the kitchen for starching. You'd boil a kettle of water, then dissolve the starch into a large bowl, dip each garment into it and a wring it out, then take them all out back to be hung up.

One way or another the laundry would get dry, unpegged, rough-folded and back into the laundry baskets. All this was just part one. Part two was this: Every single item that you'd washed now had to be ironed—there were no dryers then, nor steam irons, nor drip-dry fabrics. First everything had to be dampened slightly. You'd lay out a sheet or garment onto the worktable, dip your fingers into a pan of lukewarm water and sprinkle the droplets onto the garment. There was some art to this—too little moisture and the garment dried out, too much and it became soggy. Everything was rolled up in a towel and left awhile to let the moisture spread evenly.

The ironing itself took great patience and greater skill. My mom felt lucky to own an electric iron with a thermostat. She remembered her mother laboring over the heavy sadirons that were heated directly on the cast iron stove, heavy and difficult to maneuver, impossible to heat to the right temperature, so easy to scorch your favorite pinafore. I remember using them at Camp, before we had electricity there.

It was hard work and lonely work. But it wasn't over yet. There was still that eternal daily question, "What's for dinner?" And it had to be ready, you remember, at six!

The kitchen, where my mom spent most of her day, was typical for its time, dark, not at all efficient, but well-enough equipped. There was a gas stove with oven, a gas water heater that had to be lit every night to warm the dishwater, a rough cement sink off in a corner, with a skimpy drain board attached, a large work table in the middle of the room, and a single dangling overhead light. The dishes and groceries were kept in a pantry off one corner of the kitchen; the perishables were kept in the icebox on the back porch, with fruits and vegetables kept in the cooler next to it.

There were five doors, one to the dining room, one to the basement stairs, one to the back hall and porch, one to the pantry, and one to a tiny bedroom, perhaps intended to be the maid's room, except that we didn't have a maid. There was always a great deal of walking to and fro. Everything was assembled on the worktable, then carried to the sink for washing or peeling or to the stove for cooking or to the dining room for serving. After dinner it was all reversed: dishes washed, dried, put away in the pantry or dining room buffet, garbage scraped and carried out to the cans by the alley, cloths wrung out to dry, the floor swept.

The food was mostly fresh. Without a refrigerator, my mom had to shop often. Every day or two she'd set out over the hill, walking the four long blocks to University Way. She'd shop at the Piggly Wiggly, Fitzgerald's meat market, Van de Kamp's bakery, the store next to the bakery that sold dairy products; then carried it in her shopping bags back over the hill and on home. She'd stop often to rest. I'd go with her when it wasn't a school day.

I think it is pretty clear why we always had leftovers on laundry day!

Why do I collect so much stuff?

The table is littered with books, puzzles, calendars, tide charts, pencils, lists, more lists, lotion, eye drops, socks, my sewing machine, and much more.

I loved my dolls. They were my earliest fantasy keepers. They were such good listeners—never criticized, never told my secrets. They were my children and my friends. Pooh Bear was the most important. We hugged each other to sleep for many years. I would whisper in his ear—so soft, round, and golden brown—those fears and shames and small hurts none of the others knew about. Sometimes he would become quite solemn and insist on being called Winston. Shirley was a little bit in love with Pooh—well, who wouldn't be? She was the tallest doll and the prettiest, with welcoming outstretched arms, shiny blond ringlets, deep blue eyes, and the trademark dimple of her namesake, Shirley Temple. Her short dress stood out stiffly over frilly petticoats, flashing bright red polka-dots, perfectly matched to her sash, and jaunty hair ribbon.

The innocence was profound. The most famous actress in the world was a child. This was before TV cartoons, way before Barbie dolls, before Toys "Я" Us. There were toy stores, with skates and scooters and trains and puzzles and games and wooden blocks and erector sets, but not with today's avalanche of plastic. This was the thirties. We did have cars and radios and movies, which were changing our perception of the world, our ideas of glamour and sophistication, but they didn't affect little children the way today's onslaught of TV and the Internet do.

Advertising was just beginning to change from offering information to full-out consumer manipulation. Walt Disney was just starting to affect our view of wildlife, morphing the magnificient and alien into cuddly and cute.

There I was with all my dolls, playing house, playing school, arranging little parties with the pretty, miniature, pink-flowered tea set, going for outings with the doll buggy or wagon, singing songs, telling stories.

My mom made a lovely Christmas surprise for me—a little trunk full of clothes, all sewn with her tiny, tiny stitches. She'd made dresses, a little bolero jacket, a sun hat, and wide-legged, cream-colored satin lounge pajamas that were bound in emerald at the edges—so stylish in the thirties. The trunk was dark blue with metal corners and leather handles. It was fitted with a shallow tray inside for little socks and purses and ribbons. And—what a marvel—this little trunk had travel stickers on it; it had been to Paris and London and New York.

And there was a doll-sized quilt made of tiny pastel hexagons. I took great delight in tracing the pattern with my fingers, wondering at the geometry of it. It seemed reasonable to me that triangles and squares should lie flat and snug next to each other, but a shape with more sides couldn't—except for these hexagons.

There was one more doll, who was given to me much later. My grandmother had given her to my mother on her eighth birthday and she was now a precious heirloom, too precious to play with. I held her and admired her, but she was never part of my fantasy life.

She was tall, with a china head and a lovely kid leather body with articulated joints, so she could sit or hold various poses. My mom had had her fitted out with new, bright blue eyes with thick, dark lashes that opened and closed smoothly. Fresh paint touched up her delicate, translucent, porcelain face. When my mom had had her hair cut some time in the '20s, she had saved it—over a yard of burnished chestnut tresses—so she had some of this made up into a pretty new wig for my doll.

My mom made new clothes for this dear doll, too: a white chemise and panties with tucks and narrow lace edging; a long dress with tiny puffed sleeves made of soft, creamy, wool challis, delicately flowered, simply cut, and elegantly edged in palest blue velvet; and a hooded cloak of black velveteen lined in white satin. The doll had white silk stockings and her black patent leather one-strap shoes even had small, flat heels. Oh, she was exquisite!

One dark, rainy afternoon in December, my mom took me to the Seattle Repertory Theater, which maintained its playhouse in the University District not far from our house. *Jack and the Beanstalk* was scheduled for the children's Christmas play and "Jack" couldn't remember his lines.

My mom thought I could. So I stood there, feet apart on the rough wood of the high stage, looking out at the two or three people in that otherwise empty great echoing theater, and began my audition piece, bravely, clearly, filling every dark corner:

> *Twas brillig, and the slithy toves*
> *Did gyre and gimble in the wabe;*
> *All mimsy were the borogoves,*
> *And the mome raths outgrabe.*

I snicker-sneed dramatically and fought the frumious Bandersnatch:

> *O frabjous day! Callooh! Callay!*

I got the part and fell in love with the theater and the magnificent hoax of all that illusion: the flimsy sets looking like marble and the magic transformations of different lighting. But above all, I was in awe of the godlike thespians who could become anyone, bring what emotion they willed to hundreds of avid watchers, and yet take a little girl into their generous hearts.

I had to quickly learn my lines, get fitted for my costume, practice a boy's swagger, watch and learn from the others, and know when to stand in the right place and toss my voice far out and high.

I was becoming Jack!

There were two larger dressing rooms for most of the cast, but I was tucked into the stars' dressing room with the two principal women. They took care of me, put on my makeup for me—dark eyebrows, red apple cheeks—and made sure I was ready for my cues.

They tried to reassure me that the six-and-a-half-foot giant was really quite gentle, but I was a little afraid of him anyway. In the last scene, when he is trying to catch me, I am supposed to run between his legs, but I always just scoot around him.

Rush, rush, get it right! Learn to stay out of the way of the stagehands, to listen for the knock on the dressing room door: Five minutes!

And then we opened—hundreds of kids, all that warmth, filling the theater; the soft sound of the hushed waiting; the stage glowing—enchantment surrounded us like a bubble.

The magic is working: my "mother" gives me the money; I foolishly buy the bean; the bean grows, snaking inch by inch up past the window and up into the next scene where the man in the moon talks to me; I climb up to the giant's house.

Near the end, when I have fallen asleep on the giant's floor, something amazing happens. The giant comes home, and you can hear the sharp intake of many breaths, then a soft, rolling sound of children whispering, "Jack ... Jack ... wake up ... Then louder, "Jack! Wake up!" The magic of my fantasy world has become theirs.

Just remembering that feeling of magical enchantment whooshes the breath out of me.

And there were more plays.

Jack and the Beanstalk had been put together rather quickly. Rehearsals had already begun when I joined the cast. The others were experienced players who knew their parts and knew what to do, so the focus had been on fitting me in and getting me ready to open by Christmas vacation. The play ran for just a couple of weeks, so the whole thing was over in a month.

Excursion was an entirely different thing. We rehearsed for several weeks and I was there from the beginning. I had a minor role, so no one paid much attention to me. I learned my lines quickly and concentrated on observing these wonderful people of the theater. They were exuberant and noisy and laughed a lot, yet zeroed in on the work to be done with a fierceness that astonished me. Several of the actors had just returned from a tour of high schools around the state—a WPA project—and they were well-satisfied with their success, glad to be home and off the crowded tour bus, and glad to have a paycheck. I was beginning to see that the life of an actor was tough and unpredictable, yet joyous because they loved it so much.

I was fascinated to watch my new friends work: their concentration, their patience. The directors were gentle and thorough. I marveled at all that work, how many times it took, over and over, to get a scene right, to seem natural. I watched it all, from the first lumpy run-through, with the actors stumbling about with their noses in their yet-unlearned scripts, up to that final hush just before the heavy velvet curtains drag open and the magic begins.

Julius Caesar was in production while we were rehearsing, so I saw some noble acting. The stage was bare, cleared to the bricks of the back wall in imitation of the successful New York production where a nearly broke theater had brought Caesar to life as a modern dictator; the only scenery, a set of steps; the only costumes, trench coats; the only props, walkie-talkies—quite appropriate for all those directives from another part of the field. Marc Antony had a full, ringing voice—when he spoke, you believed.

Excursion, on the other hand, was a modern play, written during the Depression. A group of people taking a ferry out of Manhattan are in despair over their going-nowhere lives. Emotions run high as their problems are exposed, their ruined lives revealed. They decide not to go home but to sail on to Bermuda. Of course, this wayward boat is noticed; the Port Authority gets involved. The captain finally realizes they have to go back.

I played a kid with a very blonde, very nervous, very scared mama who decided to jump into the sea instead of going back. Just as she climbs up onto the railing, I see her and utter the deathless line, "Whatcha doin', Ma?"

I guess it wasn't a great play, but I loved it anyway. I especially loved the sets. The scenes alternated between the pilot house and the rear passenger deck. Since this looked exactly like the rear of the Chetzemoka, my favorite ferry, I felt right at home.

This is an old, old memory. Details blur. I don't have any mementos. I thought I'd even lost the name of the play—it took three weeks for *Excursion* to surface in my mind. Mostly, I remember the freedom and the excitement: that wonderful feeling of late childhood that anything is possible, and the pre-adolescent innocence that believes it is okay to be who you are, that indeed, doesn't even know this could be in question.

Cool and rainy, gray and silver.

Don't know what today will bring.

Whatever it brings: Yes.

There was a boy in my neighborhood that I used to play with—Bobby Benbow. His house was on my way to school, so we often walked there together. Most of us went home for lunch every day, so there was a lot of trekking. Bobby and I would make up our own stories or plays and then enact them later with my dolls.

There was some discussion and much watchfulness over the question of whether or not we were suitable playmates. Some of it had to do with germs. Bobby had been in poor health and stuck at home when he was younger—I think he'd had tuberculosis—so the Benbows were rightfully cautious and protective of Bobby's health; there was a great deal of shoe-scraping and handwashing at their house.

Our families were so different, I began to wonder how everyone, even my own parents, could be so sure they were the ones who were right. Mrs. Benbow was a lot older than my mother, and neat and rather particular; Mr. Benbow, who was the Presbyterian chaplain, liked to garden; I was astonished to see him put the dirt through a sieve to get out all the pebbles.

And they were Republicans, holding fast throughout the Democratic landslides of the '30s. They were afraid of my atheist grandfather, and my mother, with her socialist and pacifist leanings; they were afraid of what Bobby might catch politically or morally, as well as microbially. Of course, I was used to all this and my family seemed fine to me. I just thought the Benbows were terribly old-fashioned, maybe just a little nuts.

Despite all that, I think the Benbows must have realized Bobby was terribly lonely. His brother and sister were adults, no longer at home, and he wasn't active like the other boys; he didn't fit in that well. Since there was a certain respect due us as a professor's family and it didn't hurt that I got good grades, it all worked out. The boy-girl thing was never mentioned.

In the middle of the depression and way before the sixties, people were more serious about things like religion, duty, hard work. They didn't talk about commitment, they just expected it. I remember one incident, old-fashioned as it seems now. At school one day, our principal interrupted class—most unusual—and asked in a low voice to speak privately to Bobby. They went out to the cloakroom for a while, then Bobby came back, crying, and got his stuff and left. His father had come for him to tell him that his older brother and his wife were getting a divorce and they all had to be at home together to mourn this event. This was particularly devastating for a minister's family—it rocked their most deeply held beliefs. Bobby stayed home for several days. I had my first lesson in learning to respect other people's values.

At about the same time, divorce cost the King of England his crown.

It almost looks like a summer day now, smooth water, so blue and shiny, the deck drying out after black, turgid storms.

I thought it was going to be a day for getting lost in dreams or poetry, for remembering, but maybe I'll go for a walk instead.

As soon as the deck stops being slippery, I'll go down to the beach to see what flotsam the tide has brought in.

It was the summer of 1937 when we toured the Oregon coast. This was a special jaunt, not a true vacation, for we were on a mission. My father, now a respected professor of hydraulics engineering, ten years standing, had been asked by the government to undertake a tour of inspection of the water supply systems of the U.S. Coast Guard's Oregon lighthouses and other coastal installations, with traveling expenses generous enough to include the family.

We were lucky. At that time, deep in the Great Depression, few people could afford to be tourists or even campers. We had been able to take short trips—picnics to Granite Falls, excursions from Camp to Deception Pass and Rosario Beach or to Coupeville to watch the canoe races at the Indian Water Festival in August, and even a week-long camping trip at Paradise on Mt. Rainier—but I had never been to the ocean.

Back then, the Oregon coast was remote and sparsely populated, not at all resembling the bustling, hustling, overcrowded summertime magnet of today. Laughable to imagine back then that a camper would need reservations or that you could find elegant boutiques and restaurants and bed-and-breakfasts everywhere. There were motels of sorts—perhaps six tiny cabins in a row with parking in between—or the occasional Guests Welcome sign stuck in the yard of a widow with an extra bedroom or two. The eateries were entirely functional, with coffee for a nickel, in settlements like Newport, Astoria, Florence, Coos Bay; they had more loggers and truckers than vacationers. The occasional "tourist trap" offered little more than postcards, seashells, and saltwater taffy.

We traveled in our Ford sedan over narrow, twisting two-lane highways. Traffic was sparse, but you could be held up at times by a snail-paced logging truck gearing down through fifteen or so noisy gears to labor up a steep hill or headland. No car radio of course; we sang songs and told jokes and stories or played road games, trying to spot the unlikely gem of an out-of-state license plate; or, when desperate for something to do, counted cows. There certainly weren't many billboards or Burma Shave signs in this back-of-beyond place.

Apart from the lush farmland around Tillamook, the landscape was entirely natural: rocks, sand, forests of fir with spruce or cedar, a few scraggly shrubs. And the beaches, stretching as far as you could see, great white stretches of fine sand going on forever into the mist, uninterrupted by shrimpy quicksand or mud or even seaweed like the beach at Camp. The fierce wildness of the crashing, booming ocean and the hungry, screaming seabirds were nothing like the Sound. Oh, the freedom of it, the exhilaration! I fell deeply in love that day with the first wilderness of my life.

Farther south the land became rockier and desolate. We visited the sea lion rookeries—what hoarse, noisy beasts they are—and trudged heavily through huge rolling dunes, withstood furious winds long enough to glimpse the towering, frothing, wind-whipped sea.

Modern technology makes these coastal lighthouses obsolete, but in the thirties, they were the principal aid to coastal navigation. They were located, of necessity, in remote or barren rocky places, far from a reliable water supply. My father's work—ensuring that that supply, as well as other emergency and alternative supplies, was dependable, safe, and sufficient—was extremely important. When we got to a Coast Guard Station, we were always warmly received. I was astonished to hear men, sometimes even older than my dad, all smartly outfitted in navy-blue uniforms, brass buttons, and white caps, stand up tall and straight and call my father "Sir!" They seemed glad that he had brought his family.

After a tour of the lighthouse and its facilities, we would get settled in our motel or guest house, and my dad would change into boots and work clothes and go back for a lengthy exploration of the land and its water. He took the car, of course. This meant that for most of our vacation my mom, Ken, and I were on foot—quite adequate for most of our explorations of ocean and village.

But our longest stay was in Florence, miles inland because of the sand dunes there. I remember the town as dreary—dull, ill-kept, not-quite-white wooden houses, broken-down trucks and cars, tires, rust—an unhappy sort of scenery. We were in a small motel, also dreary. My dad and Ken were off inspecting things. I was hopelessly bored. Every time I asked my mom if we could do something, she would say, "Just a minute," and turn back to the enthralling, just-published book she was reading. She did take time to find a deck of cards and show me how to play Klondike, a solitaire game like Canfield but using only four piles of cards in play. I happily worked on the intricacies of this new game and left her sprawled on the bed, again deep into the problems of her fictional characters. She usually was more responsive to me, so I wondered what book had captured her so strongly. I glanced at the spine of her thick book: *Gone with the Wind*.

Later, at home, those exotic names where the lighthouses were located, still thrilled me. Named after the indigenous people or the early Spanish explorers—Tillamook, Yaquina Bay, Heceta Head, Umpqua River, Coos Bay, Coquille River, Cape Blanco—they would make a splendid report for English class. So I practiced spelling them, over and over. I wanted to get it right.

There is a fiery wolf with great Spirit power standing on a ridge across from me, a she-wolf looking at me, silver-tipped fur, lightning crackling all around.

She's not exactly dancing, she's vibrating intensely so I think she's dancing, but she hasn't moved at all.

She accepts the lightning. She says, oh how joyfully she says, "The hottest fire must learn humility."

This dream feels right, mysterious, radiant. Yet later that night some kind of pain or fear woke me, something raspy, gritty.

I was afraid to go back to sleep.

John Marshall, my junior high school, was a sprawling brick building at the far upper end of Ravenna Boulevard and about a forty-five-minute trek from my house. Most of the time, I would meet Julia and we would walk or bike together—lots of time for talking and scheming.

Of all our new teachers, we liked Mrs. Harshman, our music teacher, the best. She loved to tell stories about the music we listened to from *Till Eulenspiegel's Merry Pranks, The Sorcerer's Apprentice*, and our favorite, *Peer Gynt*. Wouldn't it be wonderful to be free like that, to roam the world, to see Egypt, to visit the Mountain King, and yet come home safe? This was powerful stuff, so Julia and I decided to turn it into a play.

We set to work writing the script, scrounged various garments for costumes, practiced using theater make-up, figured out what to use for props. And we drank tomato juice, glass after glass; tomato juice came in those big #10 cans, and we needed them to use as reflectors for our lights.

It was getting a little out of hand; we could see we needed help. We'd known Bobby Benbow since fourth grade and he gladly joined our crew. Since Bobby had been in poor health and stuck at home when he was younger, he had read everything he could get a hold of, including all of Shakespeare, so he knew the plots to all those plays. But most importantly, he would do what we said. He would pull the curtain and work the lights; we even had colored cellophane for him to help change the mood of the scenes.

With her tomboy's gruff voice and her short haircut, Julia was a natural for Peer. I did all the women's roles: Peer's love, Solveig, the sultry Anitra, Peer's mother, Asa. Julia got to swagger about a lot, but I got the plum death scene. Bobby filled in on the small parts—he made a splendid ancient shepherd and a grotesquely funny troll.

Adding the music wasn't a problem. We had a piano in the living room, of course, and my mom could play all the pieces from Grieg's "Peer Gynt Suite."

My house had pillars dividing the living room from the dining room, and the rooms were large, so we strung a couple of sheets from pillar to pillar for curtains and shoved the table and chairs out of the way so the audience could assemble in the living room. We had our theater!

We played to a full house of enthusiastic parents, friends, neighbors, and Mrs. Harshman. She was delighted with our effort. She asked us to give a performance for a school assembly. What a different audience that was. Seventh graders playing to ninth graders, with seventh graders' dialogue, homemade costumes, and complete lack of sophistication. The ninth graders laughed at the funny scenes. They laughed at the death scene. They laughed at everything. Then they hated us when their teachers made them write essays on tolerance and respect and good manners and regard for the feelings of others. We were oblivious, we didn't care what anyone thought, we were just having fun. I understood all this much better when I was an anguished ninth grader myself.

That spring, when I was almost eleven, Julia and I got the leads in the school musical, *Hansel and Gretel.* My last clear memory of childhood—when I was happy—is pretend-sleeping on the forest floor with Hansel while the choir sings in high, clear voices that ethereal lullaby of guardian angels.

It is cross-quarter day—
February 2nd.

The sun has reached the cleft
just north of Mount Jupiter.

Early winter has become
deep winter.

The next years are murky, details obscure. Painful truths about myself to be faced, confusion about the distorted images the world sends back. It would be many, many years before I felt truly happy again. My life slowly shifted away from the great hulking house on 19ᵗʰ Avenue NE and my confident, secure, grade-school self. Nothing worked right in the new school. Four grade schools funneled into one junior high and the platoon system meant we had eight teachers. I was a year-and-a-half ahead of the others, one of the youngest among hundreds of kids, the bottom of the social heap. By the time I convinced my new teachers of my intellectual worth, I began to notice that no one cared.

My mom was telling me I could be anything I truly wanted to be, but this idea wasn't holding up at all well. Things weren't working right and I was confused.

Someone seemed to have waved a magic wand over the boys, who now got power and respect automatically. When we elected class officers, boys were presidents, girls were secretaries; boys were in training to be leaders, girls: servers.

In Current Events we had to choose someone in the news to *be* for the year, to learn about them and report on their activities, but there were pitifully few women's roles to choose from. I managed to snag Marie Curie but immediately regretted it; Julia chose Gandhi who was much more in the news since he was still living.

Looking to the older, privileged ninth grade girls, I could see that the most successful and admired girls were the ones who attracted boys, those strange, newly-powerful beings. You had to know how to dress and what to do with your hair, what to talk about and what not to mention. You had to know the pop songs and the movie stars. You were supposed to have sex appeal, to be a little mysterious. This was truly important, I came to understand, because who a girl married defined her life forever.

Life at home changed too. My mom didn't need a student helper anymore, so I got to move into the big bedroom. Shortly after that, my grandmother (Anna, my mom's mother), came to live with us. The rent on her apartment had been raised and it was getting hard for her to live alone. She got the tiny room behind the kitchen—this in the house that had once been her own home.

My parents had bought the house from her when we first moved there and were making what was a hefty payment back then of thirty dollars to her each month. Of course, Grandma, not wanting to be dependent on her children, felt obliged to pay for her room and board. So, on the first of every month this curious ritual took place: Grandma and Dad would solemnly meet in the dining room and exchange checks, each made out to the other, for thirty dollars. They continued this arrangement for the rest of her life.

After a soft, dreamy, damp day, today is fierce, a hard wind scouring up the Sound, sending huge rolling waves crashing and foaming, white *horses* from here to Point No Point.

The house shudders, tremors flashing through, setting the reflections in my long oval mirror to jittering. Yet it is sunny, no rain.

Three intrepid seagulls seem to be enjoying it.

My mother was dreaming. She was tired of scrubbing greasy coal dust off the windowsills, hauling groceries over the hill every day, staring at the brown shingles of the house next door. She had grown to love the openness of the sky and sea at Camp, the intense green of a landscape without the killer smelter of her childhood. She was dreaming of a home.

She'd read Thoreau—she wanted a simple life. Glamour and sophistication held no appeal. She raided the library and studied architectural styles. She learned about Frank Lloyd Wright, about form following function. She learned about the charm of a period piece, but the Tudor, the Palladian, the Colonial didn't interest her. She read about the new ranch style; she studied efficiency layouts for kitchens. She bought graph paper and started sketching.

When we lived on Laurelhurst Drive, my mom would take long rambling walks. One of her favorite places was a four-acre tract on NE 50th Street, up in the woods past the school, just shy of Sand Point Way. There was a derelict, yet still imposing house, supported by an arcade of mature maple trees, with garden all overgrown, and the faint blur of an old tennis court still visible in the lank, weedy lawn.

Legend had it that this was the home of Upton Close, journalist, sinologist, correspondent from the Far East. He'd lived lavishly here and had thrown one party too many that lasted for days. The guests ended up destroying the house, burning the furniture, the staircases, even, to keep warm, to extend the revelry. When it was over, it was said, Close had looked at all the wreckage and simply walked away, taking the next boat to China. Later, of course, he became famous for his astute, exotic writing.

My mom became deeply attracted to this property and its romantic story. Eventually, we bought the southwest acre, but not before it had been sold and turned into a delphinium farm. Most of the magnificent maples had been cut down, but there was still one huge old tree plus another large madrona, and plenty of tall firs in the woodsy area to the west. The surrounding area was undeveloped, partly meadow, partly woods, serviced by a narrow dirt road. It was perfect. Out came scrapbooks and sketch books; floor plans were developed—we were going to build a house.

129

We couldn't afford to start building on 50th until the house on 19th was sold. We started packing, but with no definite timeline for where we were going to be living during the transition between the two houses, I was left feeling unsettled. We lived like that for a year until the house was sold and then we were out of there. Someone else would have charge of the nooks and crannies.

We lived for another year near Ravenna Park. Despite this strange impermanence, I grew up. I learned to play the flute; I fell off a horse and came to prefer bicycling; I learned to dance; I got a crush on a boy named George; I studied Latin and algebra; I graduated from junior high.

After that, another move, this time to Grandma Cassia's house on 34th Avenue NE where she had moved after her fall down the stairs. She was alone by then and wanted to live in the University District near her friends and the cafeteria and bookshops. So she moved out and we moved in.

Grandma's house was full of good memories and I liked it there, even if Ken and I had to share the space in the half-finished, slope-roofed attic. I think my mom hardly knew where she was, all her focus was on finishing the new house. The boxes she'd put in the basement were never unpacked, waiting.

It was in that house when I was listening to the weekly radio broadcast of the New York Metropolitan Opera that we received the somber, bewildering interruption announcing the attack on Pearl Harbor. Suddenly, everything changed. Our country went to war.

My mom had loved working on the cabin at Camp. I think she thought building a house in town would be like that, with the added excitement of planning her dream garden. The first plan was a lot like our Whidbey cabin: a simple one-story house to be set way back on the property under that last great maple tree, facing south, where there was lots of light and air. There would be four bedrooms, two on either end of a large living area, so there would be plenty of space for Grandma and the noisy teens Ken and I were becoming.

Eventually the house got built, of course, but what a bucket of compromises. My dad usually let my mom run things, but with this house he was adamant: value for hard-earned money trumped elegant simplicity and simple living. It would be a great waste of both time and money to build something that didn't have a healthy market value, so he insisted on plaster walls, hardwood floors, a fireplace, and of course, a full basement. Then the location had to be changed. It would cost way too much to put in sewer and utility lines and a driveway so far back from the road. The new plans relocated the house at the edge of the street, near the towering madrona. At least there'd still be a tree, but some years later it was lost when the city cut an embankment through its roots when they were lowering the road about ten feet before widening and paving it.

And then the house was going to be too expensive. The Depression was ending as the country began to prepare for war and costs were rising. So the architect, who was drawing up the finished plans and specifications, suggested reducing the size of the house's footprint by stacking the bedrooms which would cut the size cost of the foundation and basement, as well as the roof area. Gone: the privacy, the noise separation. All the rooms were shrunk a little, generous replaced with serviceable. And the only available water heater was much too small.

My mom just got quieter and quieter. This was not turning out to be anything like the house she had dreamed of, and she was the one who would be taking care of it and the family living in it.

By the time we had at last moved into the new house, my mom was becoming appallingly crippled by rheumatoid arthritis, Ken and I were in the process of leaving home, Grandma was dying, and the War had spread its darkness everywhere. She had dreamed all her life of making a home in her own house, and now that she had it there was little joy or happiness for her there. Still, she was able to find pleasure in her garden—irises, chrysanthemums, night-scented stock, roses—as well as a lush Victory Garden.

Later, after she became too ill even for that, my dad grew roses for her. He made a good-sized deck off the living room and would roll her out in the special chair he had made for her so she could sit in the garden among the sweet-scented flowers and watch birds or the wind in the tall firs that grew near our house.

As a young woman, my mom had greatly enjoyed painting. Now, in the throes of her painful illness, she took it up again. Clumsily, laboriously, with her ruined hands, she produced a good number of exquisitely lovely oil paintings. She painted only the one thing she could count on: flowers.

In the meantime, I had to grow up, and I didn't know how. We were at war. It seemed to me we'd always been on the brink of war. It was horrifying and getting worse. When I was a little girl, I'd heard about the Ethiopian struggle with Italy and the Japanese massacre of Nanking and the strafing of the small Basque town of Guernica, but I didn't know what it all meant.

Now there were newsreels, sharply etched in black and white; each week a ten-minute segment to be seen at the movies after the cartoon and previews and before the double feature. A grisly entertainment. Parades, with endless artillery and goose-stepping soldiers. Airplanes flying low to kill unarmed, ill-equipped civilians. Views of Paris, fallen. Views of London, somehow not fallen. Tales of atrocity: Coventry bombed out of existence. Tales of high courage: Dunkirk, the RAF. For a long time the urgency had been building, the excitement, the heroism, the glamour. And the fear.

Then we were fully caught up, wanting vengeance, avidly taking in whatever purpose the Office of Propaganda put forth, rushing out of the Depression blues into the high-paying shipyard jobs. All the men were enlisting, and lots of women too. Life was suddenly exciting.

High school life changed overnight from a bleak hopelessness—a time when there just weren't any jobs out there—to the furor and hot expectancy of wartime heroism. The senior boys were in especially sharp focus: they were all going to war. Everyone wanted to be a pilot, an officer. The girls were rushing off to work in high-paying jobs or to marry and follow their warrior sweethearts or to join the new Women's Auxiliary Army Corps. No one wanted to study; everyone wanted to leave. Even the teachers were leaving. We'd gone from high school being our last cocoon of shelter to being enveloped by the harsh reality of adulthood. No sentimental lingering now.

High school. It's where the melting pot of America does its melting, becoming a crucible, boiling over in the cruelty of enforced homogenization. The cliques rule. So does football. Popularity is the only god worshiped here. Any unusual quality, high or low, is magnified and noisily ridiculed. Someone else has decided everything: how to dress, what to talk about, what's *hot* (*cool* wasn't *in* yet), what's in the curriculum, how the grades are given, who will fail.

The failures fall quickly, put on a remedial track, stripped of their dreams, handed a roadmap to skid row on their way out. The ones on top are stuck with their labels, too; the popular girls don't dare talk to anyone else. They stay up late, worrying over their complexions, restyling their hair, pressing pleats in their skirts, daubing white polish on their saddle shoes, being meticulously careful not to get the least trace of white on the dark-brown leather saddle.

One girl has a nervous breakdown. She's exhausted by all her extra activities, trying to study hard to please her mother, to get good grades without letting her friends know; she has signed up for piano lessons and tennis lessons; she has a reputation for being game for anything—always upbeat, ready for a lark; everyone loves her, and her face has cracked right through from smiling all the time. She can't sleep; she doesn't know who she is. She gets her break—she gets sick. Later, when she comes back to school, she's somber, too quiet. She has to make new friends.

I didn't understand what was happening. I was supposed to look and act sexy and attractive so that all the boys would like me, but at the same time be without any sexual feelings of my own that would get me into trouble or out of control. I was to stay remote, like a movie star, to become my own chaperone, hobbling myself as though I were my own foot-binder. This shower of ice transformed my ardent vitality into deepest inchoate yearning for a fulfillment I couldn't comprehend. I wasn't getting this part of my life right. Fear and bewilderment turned to hate. My self-esteem was badly eroded. Everything had all gone flat.

School itself was boring, boring; all the light put out. Day after day, waiting in enforced silence in geometry while the teacher ground away at the D students—mostly the big athletic boys who had been held back a grade. Surely it couldn't have taken more than a few seconds to establish that they hadn't done their homework—indeed *couldn't* do it—and had no idea what *congruent* or *proof* meant. It was painful to be part of this.

I didn't like this place. I didn't fit in; I didn't want to be like the girls who did—they seemed unreal to me. The whole enterprise was boring; classes weren't challenging; my questions went unanswered—the music teacher told me I should wait for college to study harmony and music theory. At the time, I was angry; now I understand most of the teachers didn't know the answers to questions beyond their curricula.

Even the good classes had so much boring, wasted time. My Latin teacher didn't even know Latin; she was a Spanish teacher fixing some last-minute administrative glitch. History was devoted mainly to making sure we had read the assignment. In English, we read Julius Caesar without ever catching on that it was a play, one of the most powerful dramatic works of all time; it bore no resemblance to what I had seen as a child at the Repertory Theater.

I learned to go inside myself, zipping through homework, reviewing the next class, mentally practicing a piano piece, or just purely daydreaming, while I waited for other students' replies in class, or during homeroom, or any quiet, odd moment.

This emptiness is how it felt to me then. I know it was academically the best school in the largest city in the state, but it felt as though we were all being processed, turned into some acceptable product that someone else controlled.

I escaped into music and theatrical productions. I was practicing two instruments—piano and flute—two or three hours a day and listening to records every chance I got. I quickly earned first chair as a flutist in the orchestra. I became an aide to the music teacher so I could spend time in the music backroom with the tubas and double basses and shelves of slightly musty music, instead of attending study hall.

My high school had one of the best stages in the country and a crew to back it up—the Stage Force. This was Ken's territory, so I knew a lot of its members already. Besides the plays, there were two orchestra concerts and a musical comedy each year. But best of all was the Revue—entirely student-run—and I was in charge of its music. I vividly remember the orchestra from the Revue coming to my house for an extra, last-minute rehearsal, pushing back the furniture, cramming in the music stands. And Miles Blankenship, darkly handsome, slouching against the far wall, playing his silver-voiced trumpet.

I was fifteen and I was conducting my first orchestra.

Stormy dark weather,
traveling seas.

Wildly tossing black driftwood
logs dance their frenetic
elusive patterns.

My mother was terrified. I was growing up. I think she was feeling angry and betrayed because I wasn't properly living *her* dream. I certainly felt like she had someone else in mind whenever she looked at me. She still, all those years later, called me Peggy.

She didn't like my friends; she didn't like the way I looked; she didn't like the way I talked; she didn't like the music I played; she didn't like the books I read or the movies I saw. She certainly didn't like my attitude. She doled out barrage after barrage of sharp criticism and subtle ridicule. There was no way to answer, yet if I said nothing, she told me I was arrogant, cruel, and haughty. So my feelings and dreams stayed my own. I looked forward to leaving home, but until I could, I spent a lot of time alone in my room.

During high school, Julia and I seldom spoke to each other. When we were in junior high, my mother had effectively broken our friendship. She had found a magazine article explaining that being too close as friends would hold both friends back, that they wouldn't be accepted by other people. She had me read this, then said we shouldn't play together anymore, that she wanted me to hang out with the popular girls.

Julia and I picked up our friendship again in college, but we were never as close as we'd been at ten.

In hindsight, I am truly ashamed.

One day, early on in high school, when I was fourteen, Aunt Florence had come to visit, and she and my mother were talking about everything, as sisters do. They had gone into the downstairs bedroom, shed their shoes, folded back their mother's beautiful crocheted bedspread, propped themselves up on pillows, and were sharing their troubles. They had left the door open. I was heading upstairs to my room, my hand on the knob of the staircase door next to their open one, when I was stopped cold. They were talking about me! My mother was upset with me and wondering what to do about me. She told my aunt, who I didn't consider had any right to know, that I had a big crush on an older boy; that she didn't know what she was going to do about me, that I was being too emotional, that I was a terrible problem to her, that the boy wasn't suitable, and that she needed to put a stop to it.

In a heartbeat I became another person. I was too young to have any tolerance. I felt humiliated and betrayed. I lost all trust in my mother forever. I became utterly alone. Was I some sort of thing, a problem to be solved? Was I not her daughter? Wasn't she supposed to love me, to help me?

My mother was talking about Roger Williams, a senior, seventeen to my fourteen. He was kind to me, intelligent, and a musician. We met while working on the Revue. He was the only person in that Sahara of a school whom I could talk to, making life a little more bearable. We worked on productions together and had many long conversations in that music backroom, talking about music, of course, and literature—which was coming to have more to it than I was learning from my classes—and philosophy: how we know things. We talked about fears and dreams, war and life. He took me to free orchestra concerts at the University. I learned from him how to pay attention to the viola parts, to listen for the bassoon, to watch the flamboyant tympanist. I did love him and I had a deep regard for him; I didn't think it was a crush and I didn't think it was something bad. We were friends. We never talked about love.

My mother wanted to break this, too.

Roger and I stayed friends. He became a soldier for the duration of the War, then went on to study romance languages, eventually becoming a college professor.

I never knew if my mother knew I'd heard her that afternoon; we never spoke of it. I had crept away, silently.

I cried a long time that day. I didn't cry over my mother again until the day she died.

During my last year at high school, I met Alan. He graduated the year after I did. When he subsequently won a full scholarship and went east to Yale, I wondered how he might have changed after studying with the most learned men in the country; visiting New York, with its Greenwich Village and Harlem; living with sophisticated Yalies; and meeting all those girls from Vassar and Radcliffe.

Seattle was small back then, its population around 400,000, still mostly a lumber and shipping town; what would Alan think of it now? Of me? I had lived at home all that time, going to the University of Washington, my old, familiar playground. I had no real knowledge of the East coast, of other worlds.

And so my strategy was to become as cultured and worldly-wise as I could—I was a musician, after all; I could do this. I developed a reputation for impossibly high standards. I read the New Yorker from cover to cover. I got a job clerking at the most upscale record store in town. I window-shopped at I. Magnin and learned to sew in order to dress above my budget; I kept scrapbooks; I read Vogue; I went to foreign movies. I learned to jitterbug.

I dated men who were to become an architect, a professor, a composer, a diplomat, a mountaineer, a forester, an aviator, a politician. I worked with the Friends Overseas Service Committee. I joined the International House and met students from all over the world, paying close attention to the worldly women from Vienna and Paris. I listened to graduate students discuss anthropology, Margaret Mead, dialectical materialism, the origins of the universe.

When I was nineteen, I had a brief affair with a man who took me on rambles through the Arboretum and weekends skiing at Snoqualmie. We spent long afternoons canoeing, and long evenings talking and dancing. I don't remember what we talked about.

I graduated from the university. I did it with honors and my mother's Phi Beta Kappa key, but there was no joy, no honor. Just freedom.

Archaic, impatient Sappho:

Speak! Do you love me?

If not, winter.

If I'd had any sense when I married Alan, I wouldn't have done so. It makes my teeth ache to remember how young I was. I could have married a different man—the mountaineer, the architect, the diplomat—kind, capable, caring men. But my soul craved the poet.

I really did think Alan was some sort of Greek god—young, vibrant, a writer—the *Poet*. He could outtalk anyone, even quote Homer in Greek. (Isn't eloquence perhaps the ultimate aphrodisiac?) And, of course, he was *right* about everything.

He seemed to be everything I wasn't. I came alive in his presence. I began to have hope that I could leave home, especially my mother, that I could lead a strong, good life.

I started practicing music in earnest, reading more seriously, planning an exciting artist's life, a rich abundant one, with lots of friends, lots of children.

I began looking inward more deeply, traveling that life-long journey of questions: *Who am I? What might I become? What is my passion? Whom do I love? What is truth? Whom shall I believe? How do I know what I know? What is spirit? What is the universe? What does it mean to die?*

But then I gave my heart away and more of my spirit than anyone ought to.

It took me a long time to realize that Alan's literary and artistic pronouncements were acquired from his mother, and later, at Yale, from his close friend, Glenn. One day, several years later, when I was at Yale too, studying music, I heard Glenn talking about Brahms in the same disparaging words I had heard from Alan.

My brain shouts, "Now just wait a minute!" I had naively given Alan the right to order my opinions, but not Glenn. And since Alan can scarcely tell Brahms from boogie, I see where this is coming from, and the game falls apart. I am the expert here. I can like Brahms again and no one will ever again be the arbiter of my taste.

Later, Alan and I have an argument over the color of the sky. I won't agree with him—it doesn't look pink to me. He is angry, but for me, it is a beginning.

For Alan, it is also a beginning, as he turns away, retreating to his books and drinking. He won't risk his self-esteem arguing with me ever again, obstinate woman that I have become. I am a slow learner about matters of the heart. I really believe it will become okay again after he finishes his dissertation.

Now, it all just looks like a wildly mismanaged and dysfunctional life—looking for vitality and finding ashes.

One night, the fall after Alan received his PhD, I stepped into the black night, wanting to get away from the house while Kate and Martha, both under three, were settled in their beds, deep asleep. It was late and utterly quiet. The air was heavy with the coming rain, so soft on my face, comforting. There were few lights this far from town, no traffic up on the road to New Haven. I was alone.

I walked slowly down the lane and onto the bridge that crossed the East River a little farther downstream from our small cottage, pondering what my life had become. I listened to the soft rushing of the water, staring into the meager sheen of light it gathered onto its surface, and I thought about how dark and cold my life felt and that I didn't know what to do about it.

Where we lived was way out of town at the edge of the river, isolated, far from friends. Housing was scarce and expensive. At least our cottage was in a pretty spot, but we had no car, so my transportation choices were either ride a bike or catch a bus. Grocery shopping and doctor's appointments were major enterprises. Friends and musicians were infrequent apparitions.

I had expected a shared life, an abundance of life, with music and teaching and children—and the freedom to become myself. But there was no music, no teaching, no freedom. Those doors that had opened a bit for women during the War had slammed firmly shut now that the men were home, eager for jobs and houses and families.

The previous spring had been hectic—Alan had to make the deadline for his dissertation. It was brilliant, sensitive writing, but it wasn't ready. He did make the deadline, though, after several all-nighters with our friends, Walt and Yolanda Davis. Walt was an English grad student, too; Yolanda was a superb violinist and we had begun to play music together. They encouraged Alan and made lots of coffee, Yolanda typing his dissertation ferociously to the finish, while I stayed with the children. Alan's dissertation ought to have been more polished, but it did win him his coveted golden tassel. I cried tears of relief when his PhD was awarded.

As for the sharing, there wasn't any of that, either. Alan had simply gone elsewhere, becoming increasingly remote. He had understandably become completely engrossed in the writing of his doctoral dissertation, burying himself in his study, shouting angrily at being interrupted, even for a call to dinner. But that was over now, and I naively expected things to change, that he would *want* to spend time with us.

Then we went home for the summer. This was a mistake, although we all wanted to see each other—Alan was to be congratulated, the children admired. It turned out to be a stressful summer. Alan had, after all, only done what was expected of him, his mother didn't like babies, my mother was ill, the grandfathers worried. Alan shut down completely, unable to get his dissertation ready for publication, in the fierce grip of a writer's block that held him for the rest of his life.

I was broken. Entirely. Nothing worked right and I could not change it. I didn't know at all how to continue, what to do. We were living in a rundown, drafty cottage far from town; I had no friends, no intimacy, no way to share music. Alan had finished his doctorate and I had run out of excuses for him. I couldn't see any way forward.

I was twenty-seven, despondent. I thought my life was over. I recognized that I had been raised in contradictory ways—to be a solitary, brilliant, intense, intellectual woman and at the same time to be popular, beautiful, carefree, and happy. Whenever I went in one direction, I was failing in the other. And I had a profound need—completely unmet—for creativity, for connection, for understanding my dreams and visions, for understanding the universe. I wanted to be vibrant and passionate; instead, I felt utterly flat. I had come to believe I could never be happy or successful or truly alive.

I was a mother now. Alan, completely immersed in his studies, seldom spoke to me or the children. My thoughts often turned to suicide—how good it would be just to go to sleep, to take a long, long nap and never return to this despair. I just wanted to give up, for it all to just stop.

The dark, wet, fall weather suited my thoughts.

So I did give up. I gave up all idea of being someone, of accomplishing something, of making my parents proud, and especially of being happy. I thought if I killed myself, it would all be over, but then I still wouldn't be happy or successful either, so what did it really matter? I looked at my small girls, wondering how they would do with someone else—my mother? She was sick. Alan's mother? Unthinkable. Alan? Not capable of it. So I thought, if it's all over, it doesn't really matter what I do: I might as will get dinner. And so I did.

As I was thinking about all this, what life had become for me, I was getting damp with mist and cold, so I went on to the little riverside village of Branford. I could shelter for a while in a tiny chapel that I knew was never locked: St. Elizabeth's. I opened the heavy oak door, expecting to come into a narrow foyer. But there was no foyer; this large room was the whole chapel. I stumbled in, toward the dull crimson light at the far end of the room—the altar candle, the eternal light, always glowing in its sacred place. This entire space was filled with the divine presence, thick, tangible, an unfathomable abundant darkness, vibrant with pure being, with hope, with love.

Assaulted by an enveloping wave of awe, I fell to my knees, breathless, softly whispering, "Oh! *You* are God!" I prayed there for a long, long time, eventually going back home to my family, completely transformed by this vision I scarcely understood.

Feeling fragile and newborn, I explored this new realm of abundance—the hope, the grace, the omnipresent love. I felt alive and necessary, not just to change diapers and sweep the floor, but to hold up my piece of the sky. Thoughts of suicide vaporized, vanishing into the far side of the watershed.

A few days later, I went to the priest at the chapel to learn what this gift meant. I wanted to be instructed in this vital faith; I wanted to become a Catholic. Noting my intellectual interest, he sent me to a theologian. All that winter I studied with a Dominican priest, Father Reginald Maguire, a learned young man who was as clear-minded and open-hearted as he was zealous. Alan joined me, and late the next spring, we entered the Church together, were baptized and then remarried, this time with holy vows, on the same day.

Those ensuing years, I devoured everything, from Thomas Aquinas to Thomas More to Thomas Merton. And Augustine, John of the Cross, Teresa of Avila, Catherine of Siena, Thérèse of Lisieux. I learned medieval Latin and how to read the neumes of music manuscripts. I sang the glorious chants and learned how the liturgy changes with the seasons. I played the sacred music of Dufay, Palestrina, Lassus, Fauré. I read all the storytellers and poets I could find: Dante, Donne, C. S. Lewis, Georges Bernanos, Fyodor Dostoyevsky, José María Gironella. I read that radical magazine, *The Catholic Worker,* cover to cover every month. I went to Greenwich Village to visit one of the original Catholic Workers, Dorothy Day, in support of her work among the poor.

Our first Christmas as Catholics, the ardor of our faith high, we decided to go on a pilgrimage, a small one. Alan had just managed to get his grades in moments before the deadline. The students were long gone to their vacation pleasures while he struggled around the clock to grade his stack of freshman essays, making his meticulous notes and considered judgments, occasionally laughing tightly.

The solstice weather was bleak and damp; our supposedly winterized little cottage at the edge of the river was chilly and cramped. We had tacked heavy plastic over all the windows—the poor man's storm windows—which gave an eerie dullness to the light inside. The children were restless.

Now that Alan was an instructor, we had just a little more money than we'd had from his graduate school fellowship, even though I was no longer giving piano lessons. We had bought a car, not quite a heap or a rattletrap, but certainly ancient and hard to start. I was extra frugal with the food money so that we could buy a full tank of gas. Thus it was that two days before that holiest of days, the Nativity of Christ, at first light, we bundled up the children—Kate, who was almost four, Martha, two, and Thomas, just four months—with extra blankets and necessary gear and headed north, then west, into the frosty hills of western Connecticut, following the way Alan and I had taken with our bicycles on a splendid summer's jaunt several years before.

This time of year it looked quite different. The old colonial villages had lost their sparkle; the green commons at their hearts looked sodden and patchy; the normally bright white, noble New England homes were tinged with gray and had a sullen, inward look.

And then we were in Bethlehem, the village chosen by a group of Benedictine nuns for their cloistered monastery, their home. Mary was their patron, their mother, so Christmas was close to their hearts. The last few days before Christmas were especially holy, with the liturgy extolling Mary each day with a special name—Root of Jesse, Rose of Sharon, Star of the Sea. The nuns had made a nativity scene, displaying nearly life-size figures—hand-carved Neapolitan wooden statues—and it was this we had come to see. My family had had a pretty crèche which I loved to help set out every year, but those figures were only a few inches tall. This one, at Bethlehem, had a real shed, complete with manger, the figures so brightly painted and life-like, you almost expected the donkey to greet you with a loud bray or the angel to begin singing. The children were utterly delighted.

It was cold. We visited the church, even colder inside, finally making our way to the nuns' Visitors Room—a tiny nook just outside the grille of the cloister—where we received a friendly welcome from one of the Mothers. A shadowy, smiling figure behind the grille, she was joyful indeed to receive such visitors on this stormy, gray day.

I am blending memories a little. There was another time when I went to Bethlehem, not in wintertime, for a weekend retreat. The food was glorious, homemade and simple. I still remember the taste of the rich, lentil soup, the freshest cream cheese on just-from-the-oven rye bread served with vine-ripened sun-hot tomatoes and clear water from the well's icy depths. And the singing! Seven times a day the nuns sing of glory, a translucent, angelic sound, every note of which was above my throaty range. I asked the good Mother how it was that they only had nuns with such high voices, what of women like myself, us altos? She laughed, and said, "Oh, they're all in the kitchen, cooking."

Now, from this kitchen, we were brought hot drinks. Since the women could not leave the cloister nor we enter it, the steaming cups were placed in a large drawer which slid back and forth between the two areas. The nun who served us looked at this drawer for a moment. Her eyes began to twinkle as she shyly asked us if we would let the baby visit the cloister. The drawer was just the right size; in went Thomas. There was the baby, and a boy at that, passed from arm to arm throughout the group of happy women as they prepared to honor that other Babe. What an honor for our family.

All the way home, down through the somber hills, the sleet sang quietly against the car windows—snow was surely in the air. Martha softly sang a song of her own making, "La, la Christmas tree; la, la Christmas tree," over and over, eventually tapering off into a gentle sleep. It was dark, dark, solstice weather outside but light with joy within our little car.

We'd moved back into town from our house by the river and were feeling well settled in, with a new happy and affectionate baby—Sarah. We worshipped at the beautiful St. Thomas More chapel on the Yale campus; we lived in a solid house with a grassy, fenced-in yard and elm trees in the parking strip; there was a school nearby, playmates for the children, the Co-op for shopping.

But Alan couldn't write.

He had reached the end of his time as an instructor. He was on his way to becoming a brilliant professor, but he needed something published—or at least about to be—to win his promotion; he didn't have it.

So we had to leave Yale.

Alan found a position at Notre Dame, a fulfillment of duty, without pleasure. He said he was a failure, his life was over, it didn't matter where we went.

Notre Dame was in Indiana, heartland country, not the intellectual center Yale was. Alan was outraged to find the library closed on football Saturdays. But I liked Notre Dame; it was in a comfortable small town, with big, old houses with large yards, set among tall elm trees, a good place for the children. We found other ardent Catholics here, some with lots of children. We found friends.

And what a joy it was to find Terry McKiernan—the bakerman. Terry, following the Catholic Worker Movement, was a pacifist and anarchist who had found his calling to serve God by baking bread. He lived simply, giving away what he didn't need, working little enough to avoid paying the income tax that supported wars and national government. I learned what serving God from the heart looks like.

Terry made only one kind of bread, out of dark, whole wheat flour, and one kind of cookie, with plenty of eggs, buttermilk, and walnuts. Whatever he didn't sell by the end of the day he would bring to us at half-price to store in our freezer—much appreciated help with my busy life. We became good friends, and when John was born, Terry became the baby's godfather.

Music was returning to my life, too. I made time to practice; I found a place as the music teacher in a small, private school; I wrote a recorder book for the young students I taught there; I organized a children's orchestra at Notre Dame, often rewriting the parts to simplify them for those eager novices.

Then by some marvelous chance of fate, there was an opening in Walt Davis's specialty, so he and Yolanda were able to move from Connecticut to Notre Dame, too. Yolanda and I were happily playing music together again. She taught me that I could play beautifully; she liked playing with me, patiently waiting for me as I worked past my slow sight-reading skills to learn a new sonata. We loved each other.

And I kept having babies.

When Jacob, my sixth child, was born a year-and-a-half after John, Alan brought me a dozen red roses, saying, "Congratulations, you're half way there."

We had been at Notre Dame for four years when Saint Mary's College, near San Francisco, suddenly needed a vice-president. Tragically, their president and vice-president had been killed driving over a cliff on their summer vacation in the Sierras; help was needed urgently. They wanted someone who was a Catholic with a brilliant secular degree to complement their Christian Brothers education, modernizing their image. Alan fit perfectly. He could teach one class; he would be given tenure even though he still hadn't published any articles; we would be back on the west coast, closer to where we'd grown up. So we went. We were on the move once again.

Three hectic weeks. Somehow we sold the house; we got airline tickets; we explained things to the children; I hired my teenage piano students to pack up everything; I found a transcontinental moving company that would take care of my piano properly; we had a party to say goodbye to our friends.

In the middle of all that, I somehow managed to give the afternoon concert with Yolanda we were scheduled to play at Notre Dame. Both of us were expecting babies. I was hoping that our new baby wouldn't arrive prematurely; I'd been given a due date of September 25th—Michaelmas—a mere three weeks away. Yolanda had just learned she was having twins. It was the last time we made music together.

One harrowing plane ride later, hoping Tom wouldn't be able to figure out how to open the door mid-air, we arrived in San Francisco and were taken to a motel not far from the college. The motel room felt too small for so many of us. Alan had promptly disappeared into the college, needing to understand his new world overnight, with its budgets and faculty meetings and different rules, so the rest was left to me. I had no car, no bank account, and the moving van was late—there was no way to get settled into our new home.

While I struggled with meals and the laundromat, the children were delighted to have a TV to watch. A small drama: Once when two-year-old baby Coby (Jacob) was fiddling with the TV knobs, not knowing it needed a few minutes to warm up, he turned away, his interest lost. Suddenly a fierce, loud voice was shouting at him—the only time in his adventurous life I have ever seen him really scared. We all comforted him, turned the volume down, and began watching the next program.

It took a week to get what I needed, but once I could drive and write checks, I could manage everything else. We moved into our house, camping out while waiting for the furniture to arrive. The older kids started school, the younger ones had a yard to play in; I shopped at the Co-op; I cooked dinner; I hung a few curtains; I met the neighbors. We settled in.

Meanwhile, I was having endless days of false labor. Clearly the doctor must have miscalculated. Michael turned out to be an unusually late baby, overdue and over ten pounds, greeting us noisily two days after Thanksgiving, happy and hungry. We'd made it. We were all Californians now.

When David was born a year-and-a-half later, he arrived promptly a beautiful, curious baby. We'd moved from the rental into our rambling family home in the almond orchard by then. It should have been a happy time, but my exhaustion was extreme, all reserves depleted. I now had a new baby, a toddler not yet two, and six more children under thirteen.

I'd struggled through this pregnancy, depressed and suicidal. Now I sat on the edge of the bed and cried all day. I couldn't do this anymore; I had to stop having babies.

For the first time since that day in the little chapel in Connecticut, I found myself planning mortal sin: I would get some effective birth control. It would be my gift to the children I loved. I couldn't figure out any other way to go on taking care of them.

Alan, as always, was oblivious.

I was saved from this terrible choice by a surprise shift in the universe.

It used to be that sin was cut and dried, rules that everyone followed (or not). But our Pope, John XXIII, had been talking about the church's willingness to operate in the modern world; he was talking about conscience, saying it was fitting to think things through with consideration for the higher good. He said, "Throw open the windows of the church and let the fresh air of the spirit blow through."

I had learned about that spirit at Notre Dame, about love and compassion. I could let go of despair. Yet again, renewal. This time it was not only personal, it was bigger, global. Spirit was everywhere.

More than priests could tell me, more than religion knew, I saw that the whole world was sacred, not only Catholics. This was not loss of faith—it was to be more than Catholic. I called it *trans-catholic.*

I went on looking, thinking, remembering.

Who was I now?

Much frustration for three eagles.

The rotten carcass they had been
feeding on has been taken away,
moved out to sea.

There must be enough stink left to
drive them crazy.

They are searching up and down
and all around, frantic.

It was time to reach out, to do something that would nourish my soul. Would a psychiatrist help? Doubtful. That wasn't the direction I wanted to go. The finest musicology school in the country beckoned from just over the hill in Berkeley; I would freshen up my fifteen-year-old music degrees and find a place to teach. I could take a morning class while the older kids were in school, get a friend in the neighborhood to babysit, and be back home before school was out. I would find a way back to the world of music. I could heal this.

Meanwhile, the fabric of our nicely boxed-up society was coming apart at the seams. It wasn't clear at first. It started with the new war. There was a lot of confusion about what exactly our country was doing in Southeast Asia, supporting French Indonesian colonialism in a country that had been promised freedom during World War II. We were told that the U.S. was just giving advice, not getting into a deeper involvement. Fear of communism was mentioned a lot. Investigative reporting was vilified. What was our country doing?

In March of 1965, the first American combat troops waded ashore at China Beach north of Da Nang. The bombing of North Vietnam had already begun. Trust in our government vanished. It became clear that we were committing atrocity upon atrocity.

Then the peaceful protests of the Civil Rights movement took a darker turn—assassination was becoming everyday news, exile routine. Two days after Martin Luther King, Jr. was assassinated in April of 1968, seventeen-year-old Bobby Hutton, the first recruit to the new Black Panther Party, was shot while surrendering to the Oakland police. I was shocked by the incongruity of reading those appalling headlines as I walked to my ancient music class, through the furor growing on campus—a clash of centuries that left me questioning what I was doing.

The draft finished off any hope of trust, dividing us sharply along lines of race and money, of protesting college students and the more "patriotic" working class. Draft boards had great power—deferrals were given to college students and to the rich. Conscientious objectors who couldn't get deferrals went into exile or to jail. The war was being fought mostly by men from rural towns and farming communities, from poor and working-class families—their families had to be patriotic, to justify those terrible gold stars.

The children began running away, to Haight-Ashbury, or to the communes that were springing up everywhere. Then the children—the children—my sweet fifteen-year-old daughter—began to sing:

> *Where have all the flowers gone, long time passing?*
> *Where have all the flowers gone, long time ago?*
> *Where have all the flowers gone?*
>
> *Young girls have picked them everyone*
> *Oh, when will they ever learn?*
> *Oh, when will they ever learn?*
>
> *Where have all the soldiers gone, long time passing?*
> *Where have all the soldiers gone, long time ago?*
> *Where have all the soldiers gone?*
>
> *Gone to graveyards, everyone*
> *Oh, when will they ever learn?*
> *Oh, when will they ever learn?*

The poignant, harsh beauty of it still undoes me entirely.

Now, looking back, it is history, an ugly, ugly story. At the time, it felt like civil war or apocalypse; no one could guess the outcome, but we did know we'd lost all hope of innocence, that nothing would ever be the same again. We survived, vastly changed.

It was a terrible time for raising children entering such a world. We were all stunned and depressed. The careful, detailed blueprint for growing up that was handed out in the fifties, complete with family barbecues and gray flannel business suits, wasn't working any more. The young had other ideas, they were living in new ways and banding together to do it, looking for peace, freedom, social justice. They left school, ran away, lived out of VW's, sang songs for their dinners or foraged in dumpsters, staged protests and sit-ins, invented ceremonies, started new political parties, and gathered for immense outdoor musical events.

By the seventies, I had become immersed in political protest. My life was a great sea of meetings: school board meetings, political action meetings, county supervisor meetings, meetings of the Human Relations Committee the supervisors appointed to deal with it all; meetings of citizens' action groups, meetings with the police force, the jail-keepers, the numerous school superintendents; then meetings of support groups for families of conscientious objectors, meetings of support groups to raise women's consciousness, meetings of support groups for everything. And the planning meetings for all this.

Race mattered. The decimated indigenous people and the people who had been brought here as slaves were taking control of their own lives. Harsh and clear. No help wanted from whites. They would get it right themselves. Go home and wake up your own communities.

Non-violence workshops were given, position papers written. There were many marches, protests, sit-ins, and occupations. And terribly—riots, conflagrations, unjust incarcerations, and illegal activities by the FBI covered up with "official" lies.

The Black Panthers in Oakland were seeing to it that all the children had breakfast. Alcatraz was occupied by the families of the American Indian Movement, their children now playing among the old jail cells.

In his 1980 speech, "Europe Must Die," the late Russell Means, Oglala Dakota, summed it all up with superb clarity: "We are resisting being turned into a national sacrifice people. ... The European materialist tradition of despiritualizing the universe is very similar to the mental process which goes into dehumanizing another person so that it becomes virtuous to destroy the planet. ... The costs of this industrial process are not acceptable to us."

I, too, survived, vastly changed.

In the midst of all this upheaval, my mother died.

The last chapter of her life was grueling—fifteen years of unrelieved pain and disfigurement, the loss of her dreams, all her independence, and finally, even hope. The form her rheumatoid arthritis took was particularly difficult. Sometimes a person may have a single attack and be left crippled; in my mother's case there was wave after wave of fever and flu-like symptoms. When an attack subsided, she would slowly work her way from being completely bedridden to being able to sit in her rolling chair and even take a few steps. Then another attack and start all over. Some of the treatments, such as gold shots, caused severe reactions and further compromised her immune system.

My father's life was completely changed, too. He got help—a cleaning woman, a visiting nurse—but mostly he was the one who cared for my mother. He applied his ingenuity to making life easier for her: he put long handles on all the faucets and door knobs; he sawed down a kitchen chair and put it on a platform with rollers so she could get around the house more easily; and of course, he gardened for her, becoming quite the expert on roses. He'd leave the house just long enough to give his lectures at the University or shop for food. Once in a while he would go out for an hour in the evening just to stroll down the avenue, window shopping, but even this brief break made my mother anxious.

Most of my mom's friends were busy with their own lives, or they were uncomfortable with her illness and stayed away. But there was one friend, Edna Smith, who loyally came twice a week for all those years, bringing magazines and stories, a home-baked apple pie, a little fresh air.

My family, at the best of times, was not well-connected or expressive emotionally. Emotions were thought to be entirely too personal and private. Expressing anger was certainly not ever even a consideration. Yet, my mother must have been angry; she must have felt betrayed by life. I would have been, but I never knew—she never said. She was certainly ripe for some sort of psychosomatic illness.

It started during World War II, in the '40s. I remember my mother showing a painfully swollen finger to her sister, Florence, at Thanksgiving. I think there were several things that didn't precisely cause this illness but predisposed her to it. My mother was a profoundly conscientious woman. Almost nothing about her life at that time was something she truly wanted or enjoyed. During the war she had started to teach again, working as a part-time substitute, but she juggled that with caring for her mother, who was ailing and elderly and living with us full-time; helping Florence who was dying of leukemia; worrying terribly about Ken off at war; and dealing with me, an angry, hostile, and stubborn teenager. She was carrying all this heavy emotional stuff without any support, silently and alone as she had learned how to be from her mother before her, trying to keep it from affecting the rest of us. And we all were expected to act *normal*, as though we somehow didn't notice.

Add to all that her childhood growing up in Butte where the copper smelter killed every living green thing. What must it have done to the children? She already had a severe thyroid problem. Now, I think her sister's leukemia and her rheumatoid arthritis were not so much genetic dispositions as environmental ones.

It was a morning in July of 1965 when my mother died, four months after the bombing of Vietnam began; I was thirty-eight years old. She was sitting on her bed, putting on her shoes, when her heart simply stopped. There it ends for that noble and beautiful woman.

My mom had fallen deeply and passionately in love with this west-facing land on the edge of the island. It must have helped fill the empty, aching places she had inside from growing up in a land where the copper smelter killed all vegetation—not even a blade of grass could grow—and growing up in such a bleak place without a father. She came here joyfully year after year, even, or perhaps especially, after she was crippled. Her dying wish was for her ashes to be scattered on the outgoing tide.

So a week after she died, late on a fair morning, Ken silently put the rowboat into the water and rowed our father and me farther out than I had ever been before—a slow, strong rhythm—my father's face so bleak, so frozen as slowly he gave her ashes over to the ebbing tide.

On the return trip home, my father asked me to sit in the front seat—my mother's place. We stopped near a pasture to greet a neighbor, Leon Burley, who mistook me for my mother. My father, scarcely audible, said we'd just come from putting her ashes to rest, and quickly drove on to catch the ferry.

Did this woman deserve to die so desolate? After the ravishing of her spirit from the Second World War and its atomic bomb, whatever shards of faith remained were annihilated during her last grim struggle with the pain and incapacity of rheumatoid arthritis. Toward the end of her life she told me that for all those pain-wracked years, with their long sleepless nights, she'd had lots of time lying there to wonder about it all. She felt not so much that the world was being run badly as that it wasn't being run at all. She had looked and looked for God, but there was nothing out there. No meaning. No purpose. Nothing.

I so long to hug her and hold her and love her and tell her that's not how Spirit works, to show her what I've learned, to share a glimpse of the glory. But who am I to tell her this? We stand in different places; we are looking at different facets of the crystal; we see with such different eyes. The only way she could be freed from her despair was to enter Eternity.

Oh, Mother!

Requiem

He loved her quiet richness,
    the intensity of her dreams
        and her burnished chestnut hair.

He gave her all his shy security
    and watched her lay her dreams
        over their children
            and the strong lifting trees,
    even the rhythms of the ocean
    and the fierce close stars,
        the promise of the small seed,
            and the poems that love the soul.

Yet all the brilliance of her weaving
    was held fast in his pale and sinewy warp
    and her voice faltered
        to see the gloomy shroud.

With spirit stripped she could not laugh
    nor find hope to ease his heart.

Loyal, mute,
    he rows out in the pallid dawn,
        gives the ash of her despairing bones
        to the ebbing, senseless sea.

The anchoress, the mystic, praying in her
solitary cell six centuries ago, reveals that,

*Truth sees God and wisdom
contemplates God, and from
these two comes the third, a holy
and wonderful delight in God,
who is love.*

And that,

*All shall be well, and all shall be well,
and all manner of thing shall be well.*

Philosophy is blind; it is man-thought, never seeing that it is half empty. For thousands of years of civilization no one has wanted to know what women were thinking. The Greeks and Romans, the Arabs, the Christian Fathers, the thinkers of the Age of Reason—all misogynists speaking for the human race, sure that half the race is not fully human, claiming it is their natural right to have all the power, all the money, all the respect, all that matters. Women have been erased.

Growing up in such a culture, how was I supposed to think? Shall I think like a man? Become his adjunct and prop? Be complementary? Or merely ornery and opposite? Shall I hate? Envy? Fear? Separate? Withdraw? Who are my mentors? How shall I know whom to trust?

I was told about hard work and the value of getting ahead, but this is the worm's-eye view; I want the whole picture. I also want to be loved.

This becomes costly.

Managing to keep my integrity, even costlier.

All my life I have liked to watch the cycles of the earth. I grew up watching the tides swell and ebb, shifting later and later every day as they chased the moon. Astronomy fascinated me. When I was ten, I took an alarm clock, along with my sleeping bag, down to the beach where I woke myself up every two hours. I wanted to see for myself how the Big Dipper circled the North Star all night.

So how *do* I know things? Asking this became crucial during the great cultural shifts brought on by the Vietnam War. How *do* I *know*? Well, someone told me. How did they know? Someone told them, and so on, back to ancient times. How does it start, then, this knowing? Beliefs accumulate; perceptions shift. It was becoming clear to me that the people who were trying to run my spiritual and cultural life, while strong in their certainty and arrogance, didn't really know either. I wanted to see for myself, just like when I was ten.

I wanted to *know* in all the ways I could, not just with the power of reason, but with the emotional part, the intuitive part, where things just *feel* right. How do things change? How do we handle contradiction? Paradox? Why does it feel so right when indigenous people speak of respecting the earth, making our culture's view of its exploittation seem thin and inadequate?

And so these stories are dense; this is my whole life here.

Poets know.

Scientists objectify: explaining,
predicting, but artists—musicians,
sculptors, poets, storytellers—*know*.

Beauty is the mathematical balance of
the universe, all coming to us in light.

I started to compose music almost by accident.

This was the early seventies; the world was still simmering with the rage of denied civil rights, the deep hurt of too many assassinations, the raw aftermath of an ugly war. We were living through a long, hard earthquake. And the women were waking up, taking back their lives, their spirits, learning who they could be as authentic human beings, first-hand, out of the shadow.

Yet I was at a standstill.

It was clear the gods weren't planning on my becoming a professor of eighteenth-century music, the dream I'd returned to after fifteen years. Doubly hard to give up, I think, having deferred it so long. For three years I poured out letters and resumés, reaching out to any college or conservatory within a ninety-minute commute from my family and home in Walnut Creek. Nothing. Enrollments were shrinking badly; the demographics were against me.

I was invited to two interviews in all that time. One was a temporary position at the community college, a no-go from the start. They chatted amiably for a while, then said I was overqualified and that I would disturb the balance of the department, that my degree from Berkeley (which *did* overshadow theirs) worked against me, since, if I were any good, I would have gotten somewhere by now. They hired a young man straight out of college. The second interview was heart-breaking. A small Catholic college wanted exactly what I could offer— a focus on eighteenth-century keyboard music. It was a chance to play a couple of recitals a year, perhaps some chamber music. The head of the department, a Dominican sister a little older than myself, said graciously that she liked me and would have enjoyed working with me. However, the times were changing, and her department badly needed to hire someone with a PhD to give a boost to their professional standing—no one presently teaching there had one. A young man with a brand new PhD from Michigan was duly hired.

I hadn't done much playing while I was in school—not enough time for *everything*—so now, turned away once more, I began redeveloping my keyboard skills. I had always been deficient in what is called *touch,*

I'd look at my hands while playing—the visual was stronger than the tactile. This meant I was a poor sight reader, so I had to memorize everything and practice hard to learn pieces. I had learned a great deal from teaching students to play, so I decided I would become my own student. I got out all my primary grade books and started at the beginning, eyes glued to the music, forcing myself to feel my way like a blind woman. In the beginning I couldn't play the simplest chord—how was it that none of my teachers had ever noticed? Slowly, slowly, I learned what I wanted; it was like throwing crutches away.

I started playing music with friends again. I organized a Baroque group: flute, violin, cello, with myself at the harpsichord. Handel, Corelli, Telemann, Johann Sebastian Bach, Karl Philipp Emmanuel Bach—what glorious music we played. We called our group the Avalon Court Players, after the street where I lived.

For several years I played with the Diablo Symphony. Sometimes there would be a part for harpsichord or piano; once, the celeste, but usually I got the odd percussion parts—cymbals, chimes, bass drum, gong, triangle, glockenspiel—all lots of fun. These instruments aren't so hard to play, but it is critical to be able to come in at the exact right time with a noticeable crash of sound or a delicate *ting* or a lovely, reverberating *gong*.

I was also playing once a week or so with a friend, Bianca Lord. She was quite musical and had specialized as a eurythmics teacher, so was experienced at improvisation. Since she was a pianist too, we played four-hand duets—Mozart, Schubert, Ravel. When I began playing the flute again, we switched to flute and piano sonatas—Bach, Schubert, Debussy, Poulenc, Piston, Hindemith. We both also liked modern music a lot—it is quite particular to each instrument's personality or quirkiness, encouraging them to talk or dance together while keeping their own individuality.

Bea was also a composer and belonged to a local composers' group, which provided encouragement to its members, as well as a monthly musicale. She asked me to play for them and to try my hand at composing. We played a handsome program: a Schubert Sonatina, the Bach Sonata in G, and the Poulenc Sonata—all for flute and piano. So far so good. But now I had to figure out how to write something, preferably in time for the last concert in the spring.

All my life I'd been working at the other end of music, analyzing, organizing, interpreting. I'd been told I was good at analysis, that I had a mathematical mind, a man's mind, even. This meant I couldn't be creative, which was impulsive, intuitive, passionate, and irrational. Well, I wonder who decides these things. After all, I clearly have a woman's mind, so perhaps there was room for creativity as well. If I could take the pieces apart, I could put them back together again, but in a new way. I had all the sounds of the orchestra in my mind.

I also had one huge advantage—I was a failure. I had no professional position to uphold. I didn't have to care what the musicologists or all the professors at Berkeley thought. I was free of the chill grip of the academic world. There was no correct way to do this. I could write whatever I wanted. I would write something *I* wanted to hear. This wasn't going to be according to McKay or Hindemith, not the way I'd learned from them in school; it wasn't going to be in the style of Copland, Bartok, or Stravinsky either. The form would be organic and random, recurring pieces of patterns, irregular yet balanced, like dendrites, fractals, clusters, patterns of chaos, a patchwork quilt. Relationships would be formed by allusion and cellular transformation, like that found in Debussy's late piano etudes: tiny cells burbling into motifs undergoing continuous alteration, like water, light, wind.

I had already been thinking about Orpheus, the musician-god, and how little we knew about the woman in the myth, his beloved Eurydice. Trekking up and down the tide flats the summer before, gazing at the mountains, I pondered the purpose of Eurydice's life: Was it just to die so that Orpheus could have his underworld fiasco? What kind of love is that?

And so, as sounds were beginning to form—flutes, horns, a harp, and always, the drumming, and eerie, archaic sounds from the beginning of time, rhythms from the moon and tides, the poignant cry of the loon—I knew I was going to go back and find Eurydice.

To understand her, I decided she needed to leave Greece, go global. She became Yurdah, Everywoman; and Orpheus became Orastel, the Poet. Yurdah dies because Orastel takes the urn of life from her. The wheel of the universe stops turning. She deals with death in her own way, along with some help from her sisters.

It would be a dance, perhaps a suite of dances, but not that long. Once I had let the dancers into my mind, ideas simply blazed. I had no control over the vision—it developed of its own accord, as something that *had* to be. Now I understood how a sculptor is said merely to free the form that's within the stone. I don't remember exactly when I knew that there would be a great wheel at the back of the stage, slowly, slowly turning, that it was the wheel of the universe, that the work was to be called *Tropos: The Sacred Wheel.* It was before I knew that the principal dancers could not be silent—they would sing. Or that they would wear partial masks that intensify the character and universalize it. Or that what I had a hold of was not a story or a fantasy, but a myth, the great myth of life's returning. It was no longer a Greek myth—it had been transformed into a myth for our own future, and it had moved to Puget Sound and Haida and Kwakiutl country. And the women were at the heart of it.

In that first dance, the Introduction, no one is singing yet—the myth is but a gossamer hint; there are a mere handful of instruments; there are only two dancers; it is all just the beginning of an idea. The dancers complement each other, one fair, one dark, one in colors of the sun, the other, of the sea. Each dances with a hoop, foreshadowing the wheel. The music is simultaneously dissonant and archaic, a newly imagined Gregorian chant, but with native drumming—irregular, insistent. It ends with two horns tracking each other at that most ancient of musical intervals: the perfect fifth.

And so it happened. Parts were copied, hoops made. My daughter, Mar, who had been dancing since she was a baby, even before she could walk, choreographed a simple, elegant dance, with hoops and long scarves of softly shimmering fabric. Friends from the orchestra played the music; I directed it. It was a particularly fine performance, and well-received.

Life was moving in an entirely new direction. I was a composer!

This morning is flooded
with a bright cloud of gulls
doing their exhilarating sky dance
on the freshening wind.

Summertime at Camp—a time I savor, the thinking time, the ocean and star time, the endlessness turning into the now. We make a fire, cook some fresh-caught fish and share it, and talk, or just watch quietly while the twilight dwindles and the water moves out, still and somber, keeping a little light against the cool dark.

I remember my people here.

This place is built on dreams. In a corner where the two sliding windows look out to sea, my mother tacked up on the cedar panels two pictures cut from magazines.

One is a garden-dark blur of romance—a filmy-dressed, faceless woman being wooed by an equally faceless dark haired man, the arched, moss-hung branches of ancient trees framing the white Southern pillars of a classic portico, lit by the same spill of moonlight that glances across the woman's white organdy onto the fountain's mock god with the twin pipes. There is a sundial. There is a lot crammed into that 3 x 5 curling, fading bit of forty-year-old cutting—was it perhaps the advertisement for diamonds?

The other picture is a trifle larger, all golden and sea green. It shows a dark-haired knight with his sword pointing to the ground, his mail shining under a golden garment and girdle; he has stopped next to an immense oak tree as shafts of heavenly radiance illumine a golden-haired girl, slim in a sea-colored gown, who has lowered her cloak, also golden, in a gesture of offering. The picture is bordered in an elaborate leafy design, twining and repetitive. One edge curls enough to read the back—an exhortation to take chapped hands seriously and use Hinds' Cream.

Two yellow thumbtacks have rusted in the sea air.

Near these fragile messages from my childhood, I pinned a postcard. It is a sharply photographed dragon, huge, bluish, and of great age; actually not really a dragon but a Chinese dog, fierce in its antiquity, knowing and immediate. I set it there to guard those shards of death-dreams and to remember courage. It faces west.

I wake up to the shrieks of a hundred seagulls diving and chasing after herring. Soft light filters through the unbleached muslin curtains I made four summers ago. I pull them back to look out at the new day, the light soft on the cabin here under the hill, but sharp blue and white on the Sound, hot-looking already on the lightly steaming tide flats. Far out, a tug is pulling its huge load determinedly northward.

The gulls stop suddenly, briskly leaving—the fish have gone too deep. Now I hear the low throb of the tug's engine and new sounds: stealthy footsteps creaking on the deck, whispers. The boys have slipped quietly out of their sleeping bags and are picking their way across the barnacle rocks, then racing ahead on the flats to see if there are any crabs in the trap. I slip on my Penney's work shirt and jeans. I always feel good in this soft, blue shirt and today is a day for feeling good.

The kitchen is chilly—a wonderful early morning feeling, empty and still quiet. I draw the icy spring water for coffee and start the fire. I like to do this. The stove is black and strong. I shake down the ashes and open the drafts, lift off the heavy iron circles, and choose my kindling. I lay this carefully on the twisted paper, hunt up the big wooden matches and watch their tiny lights grow and leap through the lacings of wood. Quickly now, I lay on two pieces of smooth, gray driftwood and close the covers. I listen for the crackling of the tiny flames, dreaming awhile, until the fire is drawing strongly, and then, satisfied, I carefully turn down the chimney damper.

Oh how the water is cold! I run up the beach, scuffing the incoming tide's edge, relishing the tiny pain of small rocks, dancing through the fronds of seaweed—leathery lace of red, filmy green bit—and tiny darting fish. I plunge into the biting cold, swim hard until I'm warm; I taste the good rich salt taste, fight past an icy current, and float up in the smooth slate-gray swells. It is a forever kind of day, light and hot, the waves lapping gently, the sea soft and gleaming; a bedazzled glittering streak of fierce brightness reaches off to the milky haze across the Sound.

I stroke out to deeper water and lie there, quiet and alone. Trembling a bit, I start to remember—remember—and remember. Down through the light-shot moving sea, the memories settle in a last ripple of warmth from the tidal sands that were so sun-hot and solid just a few hours ago.

But it's hard work swimming back against the current today. There's a sudden rush of sound as the beach is alive with breakers from some ship gone past. The children shriek on their crazy-moving logs and rafts, the water frothy white now. Further out, the seagulls scream and swoop after a school of herring. The sun feels good.

I go into the back room and a strip, dripping on the rough boards. Over the sink there is an old-fashioned beveled mirror, a deep oval, hung between the raw studs. It gives back the dim reflection of my glowing ripe body—full, a little past prime, past motherhood, rich in loving and knowing. I am forty-seven. I have been alive a long time. My hair is silky and long, gleaming a dark gold, not yet lightened with white. I think about all the times I've looked at myself in a mirror, wondering at my self-consciousness, wishing I looked different. Today I like myself and I am surprised.

I sit on the deck and watch the fog
shroud the horizon until the sky is a
swelling sea and the boats floating
far out are like birds in the sky.

It is so beautiful here. All the signs and portents are splendid. I arrived at sunset with my family, just catching the ferry we wanted—the Rhododendron. The moon was rising, pale and full, just north of a bright strawberry pink mound of flowing snow—Mount Rainier. We could see Mount Baker as we crossed Possession Sound and then the great, familiar Olympics, crumpled layer upon layer, with mist rising from the valleys and the ridges, stark in the streaming sunset. The tide was just turning. We have a pretty, sandy beach this year.

When I went for a long walk on the tide flats to dig for clams, ideas came flooding in—songs, sounds. The writing will flow. I know I will find my own rhythms.

I submerge slightly into family matters and go dull with blankness; I am afraid of being lost; I am afraid of what I feel. *I am still waiting.* How will I deal with that first moment of clear recognition of my own time? When the wood is stacked and the insulation laid, the sprouts grown, the windows washed, all the pencils sharpened? When I'm not limited by when the family all goes off to their work, or when they come back, or when students arrive for lessons, or when it's time to eat? When there's no one to jounce the floorboards or bang the door? I panic a little.

Then I feel the strength flood inside me and I am rising up, a wellspring of creative energy. It is because of the women. I work in solitude, but it is no vacuum. I am rising out of an ocean of womanspirit.

It gets clearer and clearer how much I need a completely free space, an unhampered place to work. I just didn't realize how impossible it has been, what kind of restricted person I've become. At home or here at Camp, I have to struggle every single day just to do a little practice, and then I feel as though I've made it awful for everyone else. Yet Alan has *always* had a study, and still he takes over the bedroom, the table, the living room. I'm having to say constantly: I need space; I need room to fix dinner; I need to practice; I want to go to bed. Alan takes what he needs; the kids simply occupy. It's the nature of my work to have to dis-occupy them. I want my own place to work, a place to sleep, a reasonably clean kitchen.

The stir of a bird in the night.

The dry rustle of a frond of cedar falling.

Thin strips of icy clouds drifting over
a bright end-of-winter sky.

I look out to that bronzing sky and I am grateful. I throw a handful of stones into the sea, thanking the Goddess, asking for endurance—hope—praying for a blessing from earth, sea, sky.

I will ask for courage when I light the first fire.

After going home with the family and getting the children settled in school, I have returned to the island. I am filled with such certainty that I belong in this place.

I met an older woman—alone, happy—and I liked her.

Women here have made a clinic, called Wellspring; I want to share that. I don't want to come here just as a summer visitor anymore; I want to endure here—live, share, find old roots, build for the women, find the whole person at my core.

I know there is so much more that I could be than what I have already known. Women everywhere are whispering, "Anything is possible ..." I want to know if I can write music. Could it be that I am creative after all? Could I trust my intuition? Am I more than a part-time mystic? What is happening? I am open and intensely curious.

So I begin. I will find a way.

There is a surety, a delicious joy of homecoming. I am not afraid of being alone.

I began to develop the idea of a solitary sojourn to the cabin as a result of an accidental series of events.

On an otherwise perfectly ordinary day, Alan came home, heaved his satchel of books onto his desk, and announced, "Well, we are going to Philadelphia!" Silence all around. He might as well have said Samarkand or Timbuktu for all we knew anything about it. "Aren't you pleased?" he asked and launched into a long explanation of what he planned to do there—the research, the writing. He explained how his friend Norman had persuaded him to apply for a fellowship and to take a sabbatical. With the application deadline mere hours away, he had rushed the papers through without talking it over with me.

I felt utterly flattened. Was it some black joke? Had he forgotten I was a person, not his Victorian paper-doll wife? Did he think the children and I had no importance whatsoever? What *did* he think?

I have an excellent imagination. I knew instantly exactly what it would take to transport our tribe three thousand miles to a place we'd never been to before. Never mind the cultural benefits, the historic sightseeing of such a place, the fun of meeting new people. It would mean hours of explanation and esteem-building with the boys, of hugging and listening, perhaps watching hurtful withdrawal. It would fall to me to find housing, schools, community activities, to settle the children in where they didn't want to be. I would need a piano.

And what a job for me to get our house clean and repaired, ready to rent, our stuff stored, while we all lived here. We would have to dismantle our lives, leave friends and activities. It takes time for a musician to build up contacts; I would have to leave my students, the orchestra and chamber groups, my work with the community, then start over to build it all back when I returned.

At first I balked. Alan could go alone. He was appalled that I would even consider this. I began to soften, because he did truly need my support—he had been depressed and shut down for a long time. This would help him find his way. He did need me. I began to think it could just be done, but only if it were to be an adventure for all of us.

What if I took a sort of sabbatical too? What would this mean? What did I yearn to know or do? If I weren't teaching, I'd have some time for exploration. I didn't plan on going back to musicological research; I'd left the academic world for a more creative one.

I had questions. Could I get serious about composing? I wanted to make a gift for women. What could that be? How do people's minds change? Their vision? And what is *womanspirit*? What was happening to *my* spirit? And time, the stuff of music, what is it? How does it intersect with eternity?

This began to look interesting. Could the boys find some adventure here too?

Then it all fell apart. Apparently not everything had been settled, the shoo-in fellowship went to someone else. No Philadelphia after all.

But by then I had come to like this idea of exploring for myself. I developed the idea of a mini-sabbatical. Why not? I'd put in over a quarter of a century with family, surely a break was in order. I couldn't leave for a whole year, of course, but what about a shorter time? While Alan and the boys were busy with school, I could go to the island for, say, a hundred days, and be back in time for Christmas at the end of fall semester.

Yes, I would do this.

When that great and gentle man, Leon Fleisher, began playing his piano again, after years of hand dysfunction and pain, he started with Bach's setting of the chorale, *Jesu, Joy of Man's Desiring*.

He caresses the lilting accompaniment, lifting, lifting, until we are quite ready for the joy of the chorale: intimate, glorious, unbearably poignant.

It is at once yearning and gratitude that fills me as my heart lifts too, struck by a core-deep piercing grief, by a passion, sharp as fire, which instantly burns away all dross, as I am uplifted into white-hot ecstasy.

I remain in its aura for a long, long time.

This is a healing place. All sorts of free-floating rancor just evaporated from my brain in little puffs this morning as I woke and stretched and moved about.

The Goddess sent the most perfect weather. The eagle was flying and the heron fishing. All mountains out.

The sun sets over Foulweather Bluff now, a strange sight, so far south.

I opened the place in complete silence. I had to use the ladder to put in the north flood lamps, and I decided not to take the shutter off the small bedroom at all. Water running fine. The tide's about to turn—I must go onto the tideflats at once.

The intermix of movements of the year, the month, the day are so evident in the stars, the sunsets, the tides, the appearance of the moon herself. I feel attached to this motion—full when the tide is in, bereft when the moon is hiding—and curiously upheld by it all, as though this web were the palm of the Goddess's hand, cradling all so gently and lovingly.

It will take a while to be comfortable alone. Last night I lay by my beach fire until the stars had all come out, yet it was hard to let go. Even doing nothing, I was furiously thinking about it all.

start to perceive the welling up of dreams for the unknown wilderness it is. Did I imagine I was coming on a picnic? The pain sears through me. Suddenly I cry, *Yonnondio!*, that great aboriginal cry of grief for the lost ones; it reaches far up into the dark, heavy sky.

With all the strength of this sacred place running through me, I leap to my feet, arms upraised, shouting, *I will command!* It is a sense of the rightness of stripping myself of all the domestic sludge, the grayness, the despair of the constant onslaught of the demands and expectations of others.

I lie here for four days, stunned. My old determination that the universe yield to my making, to feel in control of life by boxing it into practicable portions for labeling, was a thing of violence. What deep folly and misery.

I cry, *I will command!* But it is not a manipulation, it is a fulfillment. I am meant to be open to all forces, to the flow of the river. For a moment, I stand tall and true, remembering who I am.

Oh what a silver silken morning.

A thousand shades of gray tinged with cream and lavender.

The foghorn has stopped; all that remains is the serene water's fine lapping and the little occasional crackle from the stove.

Smoldering all my life under the everyday way of things is this terrible passion I'm not supposed to have and that I don't know exactly what it is for: somehow to *know*, to be perfectly *with* the Creator, to see, to hear, to feel. A passion for wisdom?

What is it that is so frightening about passion that people are willing to devote entire lives, entire cultures, to hiding from it, obscuring it with convention and sentimentality and the absence of feeling? How is it that we must pretend what we don't feel, that we must be told what to feel ahead of time? What is so fragile, so inexorable, about culture that it cannot allow open feeling?

I have been told one must choose between art and children, between feelings and an ordinary life. What a fundamentally obscene idea! You live, that is all. If you get to understand any of it, hard work and good luck. If you find a way to say anything about it, well, do so.

There is a fine humming in my brain, the priestess calling down
a blessing—exalted, intimate:

> O starmaker, Ea,
> O weaver of dreams,
> O Ea, O heartsong.
>
> Remember when ancient mountains
> were young as spring grass,
> and you did storm across the dark seas
> to set time in her place with a shaft
> of moonlight, Ea!
>
> Remember when you blew down the small seed
> and cracked the stern rock with living grain,
> and laughed to see
> the baby beasts dancing
> in the shiny rain, Ea!
>
> Remember when you showed
> the hot ways of sacred fire
> to us you loved, and sang for grief with us
> when our first mother died, Ea!
>
> Rise up! You ashy smoke.
> Rise up! You raging Phoenix.
> Rise up! You beating, beating song.
> Ride the great winds over the sky!

Then Yurdah, receiving Ea's gift of life—the urn—sings in joyful praise:

> O Mother Creator,
> you set the great sun on fire
> and govern the laws of the universe.
>
> O Mother Sky,
> young and solitary, guide to the stars,
> you sleep in the moon and drive the tides.

O Mother Earth,
great wanderer, keeper of the changes,
you love all living things.

Mother Spirit, maker of souls, giver of songs.
Mother Weaver, our loving web.
Mother Healer, root of freedom and joy.

 O Mother Sea, the old one,
eternal dreamer, guide to the dying,
keep our souls forever.

Yurdah's sisters begin dancing, strewing wonderfully aromatic
rosemary, that herb of remembrance, into the air, the urn, her
shining hair:

Once you were a wet little wombling.
You are now a strong leaping woman
in your leafy green season.

One day, you'll be an old woman,
dancing in your heart, white hair flying,
remembering ... remembering ...

Rosemary, rosemary from your mother's garden,
Youth dancing bright, bright with joy!

Rosemary, rosemary from your mother's garden,
Woman dancing strong, strong with heart.

Rosemary, rosemary from your mother's garden,
Ea loves forever!

I look out at the fresh, after-storm world—
a cream, rose, dove-gray dawning—and I
don't know what I'm seeing for a moment.

The banks of light clouds are running across
in low strips, the sun is shining above them
onto the mountains, gleaming hard with
their ornament of new snow. Olympus itself
is a shiny white cap.

It's a mountain sandwich!

I greet it gladly—old friend seen anew.

Already the clouds shift, obscuring
the upper ramparts.

I am surrounded by little twinks of passion this morning. What a wellspring of peace and contentment that is flooding me. It is satisfying to work. I feel quite self-sufficient, happy to regard the pure curve of sky.

I spent today in a strange state. I'd been curled up on the window seat, reading, thinking about music, watching the sea, dozing a little, when I gently came into balance and became deeply quiet. I felt the sea moving—with its complex tidal motions—as inexorable and right, the embodiment of wisdom as it followed the celestial motions; and I felt the changes of autumn—each leaf falling in its time, the flocks of migrating birds traveling through, the different look of the beach swept clean by storms—as also inexorable and right.

I was in a place I had never been before. I felt ageless, timeless— moving perfectly with the dance of the universe, vibrating deeply and finely like a meditation. But always before I have been conscious of beginning a meditation, of going deep within myself, eyes closed, to a space at the center. This, however, seemed to come from all around me—unbeknown—and I was looking outward with open eyes, radiating clarity like a crystal.

Today is superbly overcast,
with a swift-running sea.

Before it rains, I must collect
a box of bark for my fire.

Did I suppose I was an oak tree, or a hard gem cast into the fire, that I would explode into a shooting star? Did I think I had a gift for burning?

I am a woman. I know that it hurts when I'm afraid and that loving is like acid; that my children, with their fierce darts of loving and hoping, are like crystals dancing in the sun.

The sun warms me while I watch the little birds wheel over the restless sea; my wood is cold and full of undrawn sap. It will not burn.

I am happy here because there's room for me; it is my *place*. Being here, I see there's no place I can *be* in Alan's life. Are we after all only two ghostly ships passing, arcing at a touch, just enough to catch fire into the children?

Shall we sit, side by side, angry, lonely, staring out to sea forever?

What anodyne, then? Should I hold a rose petal to my cheek, catch a child's tear in a crystal cup, run in the sand at low tide?

Who is the spider's architect? Who sings the lullaby to the hoarse-voiced eagle-child?

Is there someone who will hold me when I die?

Is this the healing I came for, shocking the dross out of my soul, tightening the form? Wandering in my inner wilderness is eerie; I know the shapes, but I am seeing them from a new perspective—that desperate space between the filaments of a spider web over an abyss—broken, uncharted.

I am stretched, honed, reaching for the bit of stone or color or sound that will help shape my cry of anguish-joy. The words are wheeling in the wind over me, like unknown birds, in a language my mother certainly never taught me.

I am alone alone alone.

High tide's flotsam gift,
earth-bound tree's bone,
stranded, inert,
remembers flights of birds.

I have become entranced by the complexity of natural rhythms. I walked down to the little burn and sat listening to its delicate splash, intermixed with the hypnotic sea rote, the dull clang of the buoy, the sparkling song of a little bird, each clearly distinct, each with an indecipherable randomness of pattern, yet held in place by clear boundaries of pitch and repetitive speed. Oh, I would like my music to be like that.

On the way home, I stopped to sing a requiem for a fallen tree, a small and lovely red alder. I told it how it was going to join the sea and become a beautiful piece of driftwood. The sea had already decorated its branches with festoons of bright green reeds.

I feel close to the primitive poetry I've been reading, so that it feels quite natural that I've started to sing to what is present to me. I had watched that tree reach up and fill out over the summer, hoping it would act as bulwark to that part of the cliff. Yet I realized its precarious position and wished it well, taking special note of its location, then, after each fall storm, seeing its root hold eroding, so that when it fell, it seemed right to sing for it.

You see what fine friends I have!

For an evening I had the company of
a tiny crab who crept in at the door-
crack, a refugee from high tide.

Every solitary needs a familiar.

Down the beach I see a man walking, he who can read a poem, seduce with his voice; a great man, a good man, the most beautiful man I know. I know every turn of his sculptured face, the swirls of his hair, the different feelings of his skin; he is a true man; he loves his children; he loves me.

But he is going away; his voice becomes a murmur, his writing a miniature rune, his hair has frost in it. Now this man rasps irritably at his children, shouts at cars and curses red lights, even trees; he is running, running; he can't see the ocean or tell me a poem; his dreams are shot-holed caricatures; he drinks and drinks and drinks.

If I call his name, will he turn, will he see me, and seeing, know me?

I'm about to jump back into that awful storm. I remember our young selves again; the power of my love for him still knocks me flat. We've both been battered to hell and back, brokenness reproaching brokenness. I need strength—the strength that comes from weakness—to stay clear. I have my own scars.

I am going back. Not out of passion, but out of compassion. I foolishly persist in hoping.

Very early in the morning I woke in the dark from a dream. I twitched the curtain a trifle to see what weather or change of tide was out there and was fiercely shocked by an alien from space staring at me with jewel-studded eye; then shocked again with flooding recognition. I flung the curtains wide to the bright, black night and sang with joy to the Pleiades.

I sing little rhythmic ditties as I work, squeezing out the blossom-scented oranges, coaxing a reluctant fire. I give fine, satisfying howls of accomplishment as I sever the silent wood with a single axe-blow. I sing funny songs—a song to my belly, waning—or an ironic lament as I think of eagles and salmon—the noble beasts of primitive song—but what I have is a house full of sand fleas, alas.

It is time to stir up my fire, to sing a song to the green wood and try to wheedle it into a brighter flame.

Time is sliding off sideways. Freed a little from the constant reminder of the clock's mechanical marking of time, I have to make an effort to recall which day it is.

The light flows.

Here I am.

After so many years of being capable—raising the children, entertaining for the college, serving in politics, setting up house in so many different places, getting up the skills to make over a house or to live alone in the country, learning to play music, earning those degrees, and doing all that teaching—it's strange to still feel like a little girl in the wrong shoes wondering who she is.

I really don't know how to go about having this identity crisis. It is different now. When I was young, I was looking for *anything* to be there, to find any measure of authenticity. But this stripping away— how much, how far? Who *is* that little girl? There she is—not asking, not trying—just there.

I am like a flower blooming in the woods. It is sufficient to show forth, to turn to the sun, to feel the heavy earth, to bend with the wind or receive the rain, whether it be soft or fierce. No one could possibly see or name or count all the spring flowers, and that it is not what they are there for.

I open to the pain. No hiding from grief, no gray security blanket, no justification, no comfortable depression. I let the pain in, it clears the brain. Joy, good music, love, wisdom—these hurt like white fire. I've tried so hard to be loving, to be a good mother, a good wife, to care. Now I put down the lenses and mirrors ... all that *trying*.

I have known the Goddess, that is enough.

So I feel content, but it is tender and new. I can chop my own wood, hike over the hill, but I don't know what words to use. I can't be the way I was but I don't see how I can be this way either when I go back home where everyone expects me to be something I used to be.

I'm scared. I'm not ready to go home. But there are children to raise.

As my ship comes into safe harbor, it's hard to ease the stance of one braced against storms for thirty years. I plan to bring it in, then see my children fair off and find an agile knee for dancing.

I am a falcon—fierce, somber, ill-tamed. I am good at practical affairs because I am strong and intelligent, but I have no sense about them for I am always dreaming of the sky.

I am a hunter of the heart. Let me go, let me go; I'll come back at the end of flight.

I will take my silver flute to the mountains and play a song no one else can hear, ephemeral as the evening mist that floats through the forest.

I will make a mandala of sand, of many colors, then return every grain of it to the sea.

My soul shifts, and it is my very self in crisis. I've tried so hard to be happy; now I want to be done with the lying and the trying.

The heron and I are gazing at the heavy pounding waters of full tide. I am exulting in the wildness, the goodness, but I think the heron only wishes he could catch his breakfast. I've never seen the herons play in the wind the way the terns do.

I make a song. It was just for a moment—it is already gone. Music is my passion. I will sing in the wilderness and dance to my pain.

Someday I'll hear the music of the spheres.

Some inchoate need stirs me to wakefulness in the flat, metallic pre-dawn. I watch the still-blazing planet set and the heavy sand-filled surf deliver the last message of a storm hundreds of miles out to sea. The movement stirs again and I recognize it: Fear. No ordinary apprehension of known or imagined catastrophe, this is the fear of the poet, the chartless one; it is the shaman shaking in awe; it is the priestess praying.

An existential fear. The burning has more than begun. I've traded lack of pain for consciousness: I *know*, and I can't stop it now.

All over the world there are women with high courage looking, daring to step outside their culture, learning to know who they are, throwing off the guides and frames, handing back the maps, seasoning the soup to their own taste.

All my life I have been told I don't see what I am seeing or know what I know. I suffer a reality shift, a flip like an optical illusion, when someone else sees into my world and pronounces it nonexistent.

But I am the wisest person I know. I know how time goes and the heart moves and how everything fits together.

And I am still here, looking.

Urashan! This is the name that comes to me here—my found name. It means lover of ancient wisdom and beauty.

The last Monday, a soft day. Clotty, light gray shapes ruminating behind espresso-black tree etchings; a small rain polishing the driftwood. I dance on the deck, I throw my head back to follow the dance in the clouds, the rain dances on my face; I taste the wet, and blink it, and smell it. I exult in the powerful, heaving sea and I feel exactly perfect—satisfied, filled, awake, ready, strong.

I feel as though I've sunk deep into the long-ago time looking for the source of my roots and found the long unnoticed living sap of ancient women still vital in me, deep and rich as womb-blood.

It is no longer enough to know that some long-ago grandmother presided over a Norse manor or that a Scotswoman, carrying my genes, loved the Western sea from her croft under a highland crag. All those veins of endurance, of fierce passion, stoicism, and hard work from my grandmothers are truly part of me, but nothing compared to the deep inside warming to ancient women praying in their own right. I've begun thinking a different way. I stay deep-centered, quiet, and passionate.

I came here exhausted, bewildered, and searching. I leave with a clear commitment to myself. I am certain of my affections, certain in identity, and certain of myself as a composer. I may often feel clumsy as I grope for the rightness of a particular musical solution, but it is the whole that I am sure of, the more so for that certainty arriving unawares, like the breaching of a dike: no sudden rupture, but a trickle to the far, soft side, an erosion, and then more, until I perceive what has been going on for quite some time.

Walk among flowers.

Go to the cool saltwater.

Watch stars.

Wait.

I have come home to deal with the ashes. If I am careful and gentle, perhaps the phoenix will rise. I'm fifty and it seems like a good year for it.

Reentry into my old world is a shock. I came home full of hope and enthusiasm for new beginnings, a more vibrant relationship with Alan. I had imagined that while I was gone, he would get closer to the boys—our three youngest still at home—and that he would have a chance for introspection and reevaluation of his life's direction.

When we'd decided on this mini-sabbatical, he'd somehow survived the terrible troubles at the college, but barely. With his self-esteem nonexistent, he became depressed, running on automatic. But now he is no better. The house is dirty. Yes, meals have been eaten, laundry done. But had they even spoken to each other? Everyone is frozen in place, waiting. Alan stands aloof as the boys clamor for hugs, with cries of "What's for dinner?"

I call a family meeting to make sure we will all share dinnertime and to make some semblance of order and participation out of the chores. We are five people with busy lives, teaching or going to school, so I try to find out what tasks each of us prefer and then share the rest fairly. Plainly, cleaning anything isn't a favorite, so I ask Alan if he would like to cook one meal on the weekend; he says he wouldn't. I ask what he *would* like to contribute to our home life. He says he wouldn't and gets up from the table and goes into his study.

At first I don't realize how bitterly depressed he has become and how much his drinking has increased. Alcohol is a big part of all the English departments we have known—it helps the flow of ideas from inhibited or shy academics; it's just a normal part of that life. But Alan's mother is an alcoholic and this is the first time the term seems appropriate for him. For a while I think it has to do with our foundering relationship. Much later, I see that there is nothing I could have done or changed. He doesn't want this to change; it works for him.

His is such a lonely legacy. He scarcely knew his grandmothers. One of them fled from the ghetto, from the terrible pogroms of Ukraine with her four small children. Years later, this intrepid woman, sensing the loss of her matriarchal power, staged her own suicide, then disappeared for days, binding her family close through fear. The other, orphaned in childhood, abandoned her little girl after her marriage fell apart, eventually dying alone on the streets of San Francisco. That determined little girl, raised by her aunts in poverty and bitterness, succeeded in going to college to become an English teacher. Later she became Alan's difficult, domineering, ambitious mother.

Does he suppose he has failed everyone?

I feel so alone. I wonder how I am going to live my life now. I try to come to terms with what's happening. I don't want our family to break apart, so I decide I will just do things anyway—go on treks to Point Reyes with the boys, go on my own to concerts or art shows, even if Alan won't. Somehow I'll get this family raised.

And I keep on writing the music.

Sometimes I go about
pitying myself while I am
being carried by the wind
across the sky.

Fear and anxiety are lurking in all the corners, behind the dirty stove, beneath the chugging refrigerator, in the distant eyes of the children. My shoulders ache from it. The air sizzles with anger from one child, a thick cloud of expectations rising from another, the third already on his way out the door; Alan wanders through it all in pain—silent, masked. He scarcely speaks to me. He won't share; he won't let me in.

I take it all—good, bad, shiny, plain—wondering if I love enough, or can ever, ever, stop the soul-hemorrhage-of-giving pain.

Yet none of that is the question; I am here, that is all.

Here I am.

Oh, but I have learned hopelessness too well. I wake so slowly, after hours of pain-filled sleep; my back and shoulders ache; the place between my shoulder blades has knotted fiercely again. As I drift up into wakefulness, I try to fill the emptiness by remembering the sound of the sea.

I feel so lonely here. I feel edgy. I am afraid of getting really depressed again—hopeless, helpless, forever. I feel diffused and unfocused.

Always responding, always giving outward, eventually destroyed my identity. I had to grieve for my lost self—who I used to be, who I never became—until it all came together in a new unity. And so I am finding ways to think and act that are appropriate to my new self. I don't have the time or the energy to be depressed. I have ashes to tend, a phoenix to free.

To *see* at all, as a woman, is a radical, revolutionary act. To concretize this vision feels like making bombs in the basement. There is that elemental fear of any artist to *look*, but there is a special additional dimension, knowing, as a woman, that I am not supposed to look, and that if I'm going to, I'd better see well, for the lives of all women depend on it.

It is a moment of pure paralysis before the plunge.

Alan is so tense, uptight, lost, full of an overworked sense of responsibility, maybe guilt. His expressions are strained; he puts people off, makes impatient gestures, moves restlessly, sleeps poorly. He still seems to enjoy reading and always enjoyed wit and ideas, but I haven't lately heard him laugh. He always had a *sense* of family, yet the kids can't talk to him. When we do go out, he's unable to enjoy himself—he just wants me to say that *I* had a good time. I feel manipulated, pulled down into a giant whirlpool of unfeeling. The resounding message is clear: no change, no accepting feelings, certainly no talking about them, nor anything else for that matter; therefore, zero relationship. So I can take all or none—this wonderful man with his clutched-up emotions; something extremely precious to me is being destroyed, our intimacy, but also my sense of feeling.

And I keep on writing the music.

The sea, alien
    as a childhood dream,
        comforts me with mute witness
            amniotic and ancient.

The cool caress of seaweed ribbons
    knows nothing of bright fish
        or my dreams.

By the time I had returned home after my hundred-day sojourn at the cabin, the shape of Tropos was clear. It was a far richer idea than I had thought at first. It had grown into a full-length dance-opera in three acts. The characters had filled out and seemed to be living a life of their own.

There are three soloists who are dancer-singers: the young woman Yurdah, who is the archetype of everywoman; Ea, both Goddess and priestess; and the poet Orastel, who sings his way into Yurdah's heart, whose brilliance can charm even Death. Yurdah has six sisters who dance and sing together. Dancers who do not sing are the dedication dancers, the animal dancers with Orastel, the shape dancers in the Land of the Dead, and the figures of fate, who dance on the sacred wheel as it begins to turn again. Death is frozen and mute.

I haven't invented a master plan—the work coalesces around the needs of the myth. The figures are living their vibrant lives in my imagination and I am truly surprised at some of the things they do. I thought Yurdah would be angry at Orastel for being left forever in the Land of the Dead, but she knows that is her fate. I thought that Orastel would eventually get her back, but he couldn't do it. And those loving sisters, oh what they did!

The form shapes itself, a variety of loosely connected songs and dances culminating in a chorale and group dance to close each act. The germ of all the music can be found in the Chord of Mortality—interlocking perfect fifths set a half-step apart—which opens the work. I would close my eyes, and there would be the stage with its shimmery imaginary figures, and I would ask, what are you doing now? And then I would try to give them the music they needed; the details worked themselves out as the music unfolded. I was never quite sure what was going to happen.

The orchestra had grown too. My penchant for many colors and lots of percussion, for pairs of instruments, and for lots of things happening at once, had pushed the numbers needed to nearly forty—small as symphony orchestras go, but large for a pit orchestra. Not as large as Wagner's, though.

I learned a lot about individual instruments, how the foot levers on the harp work to change the tuning—and to be sure to give the harpist enough time to work this magic. I tried a number of unlikely but exciting combinations that perhaps only a neophyte composer would reach for. And I really needed a high D for the glockenspiel, but most sets of bells end at C. However, I found a high D in the Debussy *Images* so I figured it could be done.

I was pushing the limits of the brass instruments as well, but I always found a precedent somewhere. As a flutist, I already knew the fingerings for five notes beyond the traditional highest C; I had played Prokofiev's *Classical Symphony* and had to dig up the fingering for high D for that, so the highest C sharp I wanted for the sea music that opens Act III was certainly okay.

The orchestra was becoming a character in its own right—speaking for itself—not simply accompanying the singers and dancers. What fun! The lines of action were expanding, blurring. The audience had already been made part of the whole as sacred viewers, in the opening Dance of Dedication, and the dancers had found the need to utter their passions as they danced them. Now the orchestra wouldn't stay put. In the Land of the Dead, three trombones were needed on stage as the henchmen for Death, who is mute, without life. Wearing black, their trombone bells decorated like fierce beasts, they roar and growl their way through a dialogue with Orastel, slides flashing in the gloom. Then they chase Orastel over the rocks out of the Land of the Dead. Safely back in the orchestra pit, they utter one final blast at the end of the act.

The flutist has been heard following the Goddess everywhere. So there she is on stage, to open Act III, welcoming the Goddess back to the Land of the Living. She is the Woman from the Sea, dressed in filmy, watery colors, and yes, seaweed. Her flute has been decorated like a splendid bird with a flowing tail. She plays her soliloquy with that high C sharp needed to amplify the Chord of Mortality, followed by the *Ave Maris Stella (Hail, Star of the Sea)* a hymn to Mary from early medieval times, with new words to an ancient song for a more ancient Mother.

All that developed later. When I returned home, I had only the first part of Act I. The rest would be several years in the unfolding.

Heavy weather moving in.

Surf's up!

My marriage has gone through a chapter of farce; or is it melodrama? I *am* depressed; even Alan noticed I seemed happier when I came home last year. I am consumed by ambivalence. I love him; I love the *idea* of him, his goodness, yet I feel tense near him; I feel so empty. I hate his guilts and rages, his awfulness about money, his anxiety in making the simplest decision, his remoteness from all of us.

And then he tells me he fell in love with one of his students last autumn but renounced his physical feelings for her, remaining a friend, consoling her when her father died. He wants me to like her, and I do; I know who she is: Kim. She has been to our house for student gatherings and at Thanksgiving. Now she's enrolled in one of Alan's classes; he gives her rides; his face lights up when the phone rings; she calls him *Daddy.*

Tense, his face tight, he relates all this to me, abjectly explaining that he's an honorable man, that he's not expecting a divorce, that he will keep his marriage vows.

What is that supposed to mean? I don't even get the indulgence of a good anger. Am I to be some sort of abandoned albatross? Which one of us does he expect to have sex with? I feel terrible.

Somewhere a thin voice screams, "Let me go. Let me go."

It is Sunday and the college term has finished. Kim can no longer stay in the dorms, so Alan has taken her camping. It is over.

It is also Mother's Day.

The names of our galaxy's spiral arms are Cygnus, Centaurus, Sagittarius, Carina, Orion, and Perseus.

We are at the far, far edge of Orion.

I am on my own here in Arcata now, my old life vanished. Michael and David are with me, shut down in their own miseries.

I found a good house, up the hill across from the redwood forest. To attract piano students, I give a concert at the Jambalaya, a local night spot in town; I join the community orchestra, find bookstores, look for friends. I join a women's group protesting the attempt to force a logging road through land sacred to the Hupa and the Yurok; I give nonviolence workshops; I go for long walks in the endless, dripping forest; I explore the wet marsh, watching the sea birds; I dance in the All Species Parade; I seek out the women, who, everywhere, unable to trust male-dominated culture, are finding new ways to be.

And I go on writing Tropos. I turn my grief into Orastel's song of love—strong, with great tenderness, hypnotically compelling.

> Once in the beginning of time
> there was a bright mountain as lustrous
> as a snow pearl in the first dawn.
>
> Yurdah, you are more fair!
>
> Once in the beginning of time
> there was a waterfall
> splashing sunfire in new rock.
>
> Yurdah, you are more fair!
>
> Once in the beginning of time
> there was a cedar tree,
> proud and reaching in the green land.
>
> Yurdah, you are more fair!
>
> I'll take you east of the sun
> to see the dragon tombs.
>
> I'll take you to the Western Isles
> where the mountains rise from the sea,
>
> I'll build for you a crystal tower
> and live in ecstasy, in ecstasy.

I feel caught between worlds. I'm on a narrow, silvery, high-arching bridge; I *must* go forward; I can't see back; when I look down, it is terrifying.

I've rejected professionalism, yet I'm not jazz; I don't like men much right now, but I'm not lesbian either. My confidence as a solitary and as a composer are both decidedly thin.

I must be quiet now. Yet I alternate madly—the awareness, the sharp dreams, then clinging desperately to old comforts.

Grief comes raging down, sweeping my soul-sand clean, a devouring firestorm; I hold, like a great redwood streaming about in the pouring wind.

Then a leering crone, in nostalgic, musty clothes, shows forth her cracked, empty eggs. I am powerfully afraid.

Send down roots. Hold! Hold!

I am a December rose—hard-formed on heavy, gaunt and discolored stock, burnt by the wind, yet solid and intense—both remembrance and harbinger of what the summer sun can do.

My voice is cracked.

I fear the music won't hold.

Strong dreams push at me, choking me.

I am serving a lovely dinner for Alan and his friend Glenn. The kitchen is the one I grew up in—with its gas heater, the clumsy sink, the glass-doored pantry—and it is an amazing mess of pots, chicken carcasses, vegetable parings, and so on.

They have demolished everything before I could sit down, not even a scrap of lettuce left for my dinner. It makes me sad, but I clear the plates, serve dessert. I have made something special, a crusty meringue, in a circle, to be filled with berries and cream. I put the meringue on the table and go back to the kitchen for the filling. I'm glad I've made something so pretty for them.

But they have eaten up the meringue and are shoving back their chairs, about to rush off. I say, "But didn't you leave *any* for me?" They laugh gaily, and Glenn says, as though he were a great wit, "Oh, never mind; anyway, you can have the whipped cream." They laugh and laugh at me, sauntering off, those insouciant young men.

Waking, crying, I am flooded with forgiveness deeper than any I have experienced before. I am surrounded by light—I *feel* light. I recognize that I have been hurt far more than I ever knew, right down to the bone, past identity, deep into the soul, as near fatal as can be and still live. I can feel it all the way through without guilt or hedging; I can feel it all the way down without fear. I can let it go now.

I see Alan in my mind's eye—a little boy, a young man, a father, and as he is now. I see him clearly, light everywhere. He is just who he is—uniquely himself. He seems tender, confused, alone. I send him great waves of compassion.

The forgiveness? It is huge, but it is not for him. He gets no blame, no anger. Forgiveness is for oneself. It is the dissolving of barriers in the mind and of the hardness of the heart.

I won't dream of Alan again.

Slowly I discard the expectations of my past life.

What did it mean to love like that and then have it all come to such a grinding halt? And why did I give away all the strength and power of my adult life in loyalty to such a dwindling enterprise?

For a long time, I felt as though I had failed him. That strong feeling of worthlessness goes all the way back to our early marriage when it was clear I wasn't making him happy. I had to learn that I wasn't responsible for his unhappiness, that he was failing me, too.

I had to find my own happiness, but believing this to be impossible, I lived my life serving others.

Now, I know my worth, my humanity, yet I feel so low.

Solitude is a dark flame.

Sailboats like mushrooms—
  iconic, hot white memories—
    inch through thick sodden rain.

It has been such a wet spring and summer; the cabin here at Camp is musty, verging on dank. Four birds—two of them nestlings—died in the cabin sometime during the spring. The drive is lush with grass, nettles the height of a person everywhere. Tough, wild roses have sprung up in the clearing. Everything needs cleaning and airing, but it's hard to air bedding in this rainy mizzle. The trail appears to be seriously eroded, but I haven't been able to reach the hill yet—first I must find my gloves and sharpen the machete.

Even so, the beauty of this place grips and holds me close to the Goddess source. The moon is waxing and I'll be here until she comes again. The beach is high this year. Ken's staked-out logs have held and the bank is not eroded any further. The roof holds, the wood burns sweetly, and the sea has not come inside.

I resist the temptation to plan an orgy of digging, hacking, trail-making, cleaning, rock hauling, painting. I came to center, to let my soul stretch out, to touch my friends. I'll wash a plate or two and a pot, clean off what I need to use, and let the rest come as it will. I'm still tired from the trip up and opening the cabin, but there's a minus tide at one o'clock and I'll be out there.

Today, having settled in at the cabin, I climbed the hill. The trail was badly overgrown with ivy and nettles; there was lots of down wood and loose material I had to remove in order to get a safe footing; all trace of the steps I had cut last time were washed away. I got the water tank stopped up and found the pipe from the spring and connected it.

While it started to fill, I climbed up toward the little house. Looking up, I saw a raw gash in the face of the hill—a huge tree down. The little house my son David had made in a spirit of pure joy was gone, swept away in the branches of the fallen tree.

I didn't go over to the site—it was sloshy and precarious. I felt sad all day. It was like the feeling you get in Ursula K. Le Guin's *A Wizard of Earthsea* when Ged's boat is lost: You so very much want it to be all right, but you know nothing will ever be the same again.

The little house, gone like a butterfly, was beautiful.

Everything changes. It is a new time.

You *will* do things Your own way!

I sang Your glory into the soft wind at dawn and asked for Your blessing, which You always give for the asking.

I hoped for that clearing of the heart, that peace, which You scatter here with Your usual abundance, like grass or stars. You didn't stint in Your everyday miracles: the living mountains, the great tidal dance, the astonishing family of plants and beasts that call this place home, each perfect day followed by another such.

This extra gift I wasn't expecting; I weep tears of hot gratitude for it.

To know, after reading the cabin journal, then spending a day with my son Michael, talking of love and dreams and the way the earth is, watching the care he lavishes on his special plants, bedazzled by his beauty as he takes to the sea in his kayak, paddles lifting airily into the dying sun; to know, after reading this rich journal, written by everyone in the family, that he, that all my children, have gotten it, my best gift, of how to love here; to know after all that my seemingly inconclusive life has all the time been nourishing untold richness.

There is a country of the mind where there is freedom and wisdom and my voice lives there. I remember being here at the beach, opening out as far as I could see, past water and lights and mountains, until I was part of the very stars.

And I go on writing Tropos.

Yurdah has died! My heart is on the line. I am exhilarated. I am shaking. I am terrified.

(Women)

> Go, sweet Yurdah, to that long night
> where no star shines, no wind stirs,
> no bird flies, where no day breaks,
> no tide runs, no spring comes.
>
> Yurdah Dayspring, go gently, farewell!
>
> Dare no rose bloom!
> Dare no fish leap!
> Dare no lark sound!
>
> Shroud your hearts and greet the night!
> Shroud your hearts and greet the night!

(Yurdah)

> Strange, strange desolate country,
> dank dripping rocks in shrouds of mold.
> Weird beasts lurk in green scum, nameless
> fish, slimy reptiles gleam in ancient steamy
> swamps and pierce my frightened eye.
>
> All, all in decay and time is no more,
>
> My only friends the drifting shades of lost
> dreams dancing in the Land of the Dead.

All morning, here under the dark Arcata redwoods, I've been drowning in apocalypse, mourning the world, dreaming of innocence, agonizing over war.

Endlessly, one war spills into another. The horror of genocide against Indians turns into the Civil War, moves west to Japan and Hiroshima, and on to Indochina and Vietnam, killing millions and half the land with the devastating fury of fire, smallpox, atomic explosion, napalm, herbicides—poisoning the earth, even its very air.

Through all this, I am writing Yurdah's vision, mourning with her sisters from the Land of the Dead. It is a litany.

(Women)	Women gather, gather. Women gather in darkness, Waiting for the turning of the night.
(Yurdah)	Waiting in darkness, eon after eon, I watch them tear the earth apart and spill out all her seed. Rage, oh rage, my heart! Grief has cracked my face!
(Women)	Women gather.
(Yurdah)	Great winds scream across the dying seas. The sweet green forests lie burnt-out hulks in sulfur deadly pall. The heavens shift their ancient frame. Stars are falling one by one.
(Women)	Women gather.
(Yurdah)	Waiting in darkness, eon after eon, My people lie scattered, broken, Doomed to endless deadly hate. Rage, oh rage, my heart! Grief has cracked my face!
(Women)	Women gather, gather. Women gather in darkness, Waiting for the turning of the night.

Tropos is not a masterpiece; I am writing a *motherwork*. It goes deep below the level of our taught culture to the half-remembered dreams of the earth of our common, shared future. It is for the strength and courage to come back from the Land of the Dead, to live, renewed.

(Women)   We are women, we are strong,
           We are daughters of the Goddess,
           Proud as stars and fierce as rain.
           Storm the dark night!
           Womanspirit rise again!

           Oh let the healing now begin!

           Death may take us one by one,
           Rape our souls and still our voices.
           Go as one and Death must yield.
           Fiery hope, sweet friendship
           Weave our sacred bond.

           Go arm in arm, our courage high!

           We are women, we are strong,
           We are daughters of the Goddess.
           Share our gifts of living seed.
           Bring the dark and sinking earth
           Our joyous love.

           Oh let the healing now begin!

While that unnamed mystic was writing *The Cloude of Unknowyng* during the tumultuous uncertainties of the fourteenth century—endless war, hopeless plague, inevitable famine, all causing enormous dislocations to the social fabric—there were many prophecies, from apocalyptic destruction and desolation to deep spiritual renewal.

No one, no one at all, could foresee that in fifty years the great spirit of the Renaissance would burgeon and change the world forever.

What greatness of human spirit will rise up now to transform our universe?

The Trappist monk praises
the useless life.

But there is no need to justify
a life of contemplation.

Love because you love.

Spirit has been running strong in me today. I played Bach fugues and Beethoven's Opus 109 and Chopin nocturnes and Debussy études. Mature works with that astonishing inner space that fills me with such excitement, such intimate serenity.

Then I walked in the redwoods just before the great storm that left me without power. The light was a soft green and thick, the tops of the trees swaying deeply, yet all was quiet below. I felt powerful and I knew that I could finish Tropos, that I could do whatever I need to do. I am rich in solitude.

I have been having visions all day. I call them visions for lack of an appropriate name, but they are aural and spatial, intimate movement filled with great rhythms.

I am joyful. It is a somber joy at the interface of life and death. November is a time for gathering in, to cherish dreams and long walks, stormy seas, the golden autumn moon, ancient remembering, old friends.

When I first embraced the sacred ordinary, I just *knew*, by intuition, by a physical, sensual certainty, that separation into a monastery or any other form of identification or division would not let me think clearly, that it would obscure the light from what I sought.

Knowing in a holistic way is slow work.

The poets and mystics have gotten it from the beginning.

So why haven't the rest of us been listening? We do everything to escape those visionaries. We call them artists or saints, we put them on inaccessible pedestals, romanticize them, admire their impossibility, call them different, impractical, eccentric, extraordinary, insane. They are isolated, cut off, tormented.

Could we learn to pay attention?

Shall we remember who we are?

This wild, vibrant life I am living now, I don't know when it started exactly. Somewhere along the way I began to learn to see for myself.

This vision of spirit is as common as salt. *Anyone* may look. I don't need the validation of an academic degree or a synod of elders. I am my own elder.

It is sufficient that I *am*.

In the depths of winter, Arcata
is quiet, utterly bleak, and never
altogether dry.

It's not quite a mist or a drizzle,
just a pervasive moisture, leaving
linens tacky, rusting the staples
in all my sheet music.

I spend the day alternately playing the piano and lying in my loft, thinking. My emotions begin to expand and I give way to the visions that are starting, accepting the fierce pain that goes with them.

I have been having intense apocalyptic nightmares, overwhelming grief at the mindlessness of cruelty and violence; at the utter disconnectedness, the desolation and madness of the violent one separated from the godhead, and the gentle justice of earthly exchanges; at the necessary involvement of all of us in this; and at the staggeringly immense effect of the violence on the children, whole populations, species, our planet.

Somehow, in that curious alchemy called art, all this grief and love become concentrated, like the formation of diamonds, into that remembrance of pain—its exquisite clear light etching like acid into the human heart—and beauty.

I had been warned to avoid distractibility, triviality, and diffuseness by my mentor, the Dominican theologian Reginald Maguire, all those years ago. Perhaps good advice for monks, but I found these to be skills that are essential for raising children, skills that are learned from the practice of loving, from the wholehearted attending to the well-being of another.

The two-year-old of normal adventuresomeness would die if not cared for by someone who was instantly distractible from the focus of work when that child was in danger. The trivial in all its specific detail and endless repetition—all those nursery rhymes and silly songs—brings comfort and security, and it's fun. Diffuseness opens the world of tolerance, of spontaneity and laughter, of dancing and telling jokes.

As I return to my habits of focus, concentration, and self-assertion when composing music, I wonder if these other skills are to be shucked. Reluctant to waste, I now discover in them a healthy resource, like a scrap bag kept over a lifetime. If I think piecemeal, returning again and again, like counterpoint or doing needlework, the pattern will emerge.

Bonus! Many patterns will emerge. Diffuseness of vision allows great richness to be found, lovingkindness shared; distractibility nourishes the joy of play, the vitality of improvisation; pleasure in the trivial permits spending lavish care over the most innocuous-seeming detail.

As a composer and musician working in a highly abstract art, I want to understand what difference it makes to be a feminist. My close blood bond with the monthly heavings of the sea, my post-menopausal elder-mother's connection to the cosmic earth-nurturing rhythms, gives me a womanly sense of the vitality of rhythms that are constantly shifting and returning. In music, this physical energy permeates the abstract with its rhythmic variety, its reverberations, its freshness of return after being torn apart through exploration and development, becoming the language of interbeing, the language of the heart.

This is the world not of orderly expository explanation but of poetry, not a question of style, then, but ultimately one of vision.

Art is powerful. Laws change the rules. Art changes the heart.

I have the power to
change you forever.

I can *love* you.

Arcata is a healing place, a community that comforts the hurt and broken, nourishes the original—honoring the eccentric, the weird. Art flourishes; books abound. Life is easy here.

I became happy here.

No one has much money. A Green Party majority guides the city council. Across from my house, there's a municipal forest—the first in the country. Its towering redwoods have become an inadvertent shelter for the homeless; the clown, Rudy, lived in the cavelike hollow of one of the trees up the hill all one school year, before sheltering in my house the next winter.

The favorite competitive sport here is Ultimate Frisbee. The Humboldt team's objective is to have fun, not to win. Once, when David, my youngest, was playing in one of their games, I watched the team stop play to gently explain this to the Berkeley team, who had become entirely too cutthroat.

And the Kinetic Sculpture Race—unique—not really a race, just three days of improbable, fantastically decorated works of art: human-powered amphibious contraptions full of families, friends, and lots of laughter, crossing hills and sand dunes, reveling in the mud flats, rowing/sailing against the tide in Humboldt Bay, and on to that tiny, Victorian jewel of a town, Ferndale. I remember fierce dragons, centipedes, bright and beautiful birds, tall sailing ships, and giant red "tricycles" with too many wheels. The race's founder always comes in last.

Yes, I love this place, but I can't make a living here. My music studio is faltering. The university's student base is shrinking—new professors aren't being hired, so there are no new kids wanting music lessons. I've rented out rooms, grown a garden, but it just isn't working. I need a bigger arena and a chance for performing Tropos.

I'm moving back to the Bay Area.

I found a small cottage in Kensington, north of Berkeley, that was just right for a music studio for my teaching, but my contacts had evaporated, children grown, families changed. I couldn't get enough students; I wasn't finding chamber music connections; I had no reputation as teacher or performer.

I wasn't having any luck with Tropos, either: Academic friends performed only their colleagues' works or the teaching repertory; opera contacts said to try the dancers, dancers, the opera; producers were pursuing their own avant-garde works. The Bay Area was a no-go. I'd already sent the score all over the country, with no results. Tropos was going to have to wait.

What were other women doing, those who had found themselves high and dry, too young for Social Security, too old to be easily employable, too old to build their own careers? I found them serving as housemothers in the dorms, hostesses in upscale restaurants, knowledgeable clerks in bookstores. Could I think of some other way to support myself? I knew I didn't want to face the practicing needed to give concerts in that highly competitive community, so I looked around, read helpful books, wrote down assets, pondered answers to the questions in *What Color Is Your Parachute?* When were you happy? What did you like to do then? Easy: I was ten and I loved math and astronomy and solving puzzles. I thought, since I have a good brain, I might be able to work with computers. All the younger folk seemed to be headed in that direction.

So I enrolled in the Computer Learning Center in San Francisco to study computer programming. To pay for it, I sublet my cottage and lived out of my truck all spring and summer—first at Yosemite, then along the Merced River—all the while studying and reviewing math. It was a rich time. I met all kinds of interesting people—travelers, entertainers, job hunters, followers of the craft-show circuit—and because I was alone, it was easy to make friends.

In the fall, back in school, I worked hard to get to the top of the class, only to run full tilt, once again, into the prejudice against women—

even more so, older women. Southern Pacific was hiring programmers, but the placement office decided I was unsuitable and sent two younger candidates. One, a man, was hired. A year later, he kindly let me know the railroad was hiring again; I passed their exam, finally getting the job I wanted. I liked my manager, my coworkers respected me, the work was interesting, I liked railroads, and no one cared how old I was—they only cared that I was good at my job. And I was good at it, eventually moving from programming to software design.

I figured out what the placement office had cost me: a year's wages, promotions, pay increases, retirement benefits, IRA and Social Security contributions—besides all that heaving anxiety. Even after I deducted a percentage for increased income taxes, it was so staggering that I just forgot about it and sent them a thank you note instead.

I hadn't realized how hard it would be, working in a new field. I was used to knowing what I was doing; I was the teacher. Overnight, I was a neophyte with no knowledge of railroading and its extremely complex computer filing system. It was six months before I stopped crying myself to sleep every night, exhausted.

A railroad runs 24/7, calculations made on the fly, with no downtime for updating files. There are files within files, pointing to yet other files, as size, cargo, personnel, time zones, and state laws vary. The train itself is just a concept—cargo with a destination—workers change shifts, loads are delivered or added, boxcars are shifted around to balance the load, locomotives added to help get the train over the mountains. What begins in New Orleans is quite different when it reaches Los Angeles.

We ran on five immense mainframe computers—the largest installation in the country apart from the military—and two of them ran seamlessly in tandem, so that one was always working even if the other was down for repairs or adjustment. The first two floors of the ancient building at 1 Market Street were given over to the operators, who managed the hardware, while the entire third floor belonged to us programmers, who wrote the software. It was all immensely powerful, its caretakers skilled. When the Loma Prieta earthquake knocked out all the power throughout the Bay Area in the fall of 1989, we were the first ones back up and running.

Still, some of the coding dated back to 1965 before there were personal computers. Southern Pacific and IBM had collaborated to make the earliest computer filing systems, developing registers and pointers to make information storage flexible enough to run a railroad. That archaic coding needed special handling. A simple mistake could bring the whole system down.

There were rich technical terms and colloquial meanings to master— *hogs, bowl tracks, beans, green eye*—it felt like being at sea on the Scamper when I was five, where everything had a special name. This was turning out to be high fun, the best puzzle I'd ever worked on.

Yet software can be dangerous. Software can kill. On a Friday morning, May 12, 1989, around 7:30, a runaway train came hurtling down the mountain canyon into San Bernardino and derailed, destroying several homes, and killing the people in them. The entire train—Southern Pacific Transportation Company freight train 1-MJLBP-111—which consisted of a four-unit locomotive on the head end of the train, sixty-nine hopper cars loaded with trona, and a two-unit helper locomotive on the rear of the train—was destroyed and two of its crew members were killed.

We worked long hours into the night and all weekend to find out why. Because the weighing stations at point of origin had been closed, the computer had used average weights by default, instead of actual weights, to make its calculations. But it was a full load of trona—a heavy metal mined from the salt flats of Mono Lake. Computer calculations for the brakes needed to control such a load had shown the train's brakes to be adequate when they were not; more helper locomotives should have been added to control the trona-laden train on its steep descent, but they were not. The train plummeted.

What was a contemplative doing in such a harsh workplace? Southern Pacific needed software with the precision of perfection. Was this, too, the sacred ordinary? Was the Goddess riding the rails? Switching locomotives? Comforting hobos? Lurching down the mountains with the wind in her face?

I learned to meditate on the ride to work, reminded by the sleepy owl at the marsh's edge of other worlds. Walking from the bus station, I would stop and talk to the women artists who sat at the edge of the street and admire their lovely craft work. The courage of these homeless women fueled a deep compassion in me as I begin to recognize my own homelessness. Sudden impossible pain—sharp, clean, that primal agony of being pushed out to the margins, of not being recognized, not being seen, not being validated, of having one's deepest core truths obliterated—nearly annihilates me.

One dark Tuesday afternoon on October 17, 1989 at 5:04, that same disastrous year, the world started shaking—heavily, uncontrollably—all lights abruptly out. I was on the bus, heading home; the bus driver panicked and bolted for the Oakland Bay Bridge, wanting to get out of San Francisco as quickly as possible. But halfway across, on the tiny island of Yerba Buena, we were stopped by a surge of people frantically running toward us back to the city. The bridge was falling! The driver just left it all there, and we ran too.

Many people decided to look for shelter on the island or to make emergency phone calls. I thought that was too dangerous—great tangles of fallen wires were everywhere. Yet I had no fear. When in danger, I don't panic, I get preternaturally calm and hyperalert; I pay attention, evaluate options.

It was utterly dark now; I needed to find shelter. I trekked the three-and-a-half miles back to Market Street, now littered with fallen masonry and stalled cars, but I didn't want to enter that unsafe, old building where my office was. Just when I had decided to look for shelter at the Hyatt hotel, a bus pulled up, its overhead sign fortuitously blazing *Palo Alto* in the now black night; scarcely thinking, I jumped aboard. I had found a way out.

The entire Bay Area was stark black, except for the fires—a lurid luminescence over the Marina area and an immense, fiery smoke column across the bay near Berkeley. All the familiar landmarks had been obliterated by the night. In San Francisco, with the stoplights out, traveling across the rubble-filled city was treacherous and tediously slow. We stopped at the airport, then again, farther south, finally reaching Palo Alto nearly four hours later, a little after eleven o'clock. I called Mary Anne—dear cousin—and sank gratefully into her arms when she arrived to drive me to her home. Palo Alto had suffered the quake less severely and her place was safe.

The next day we learned that the earthquake's epicenter was in the Santa Cruz mountains at Loma Prieta. The freeway viaduct in

Oakland had collapsed, but BART trains were running safely in the East Bay. Mary Anne drove me across the undamaged Dumbarton Bay bridge to Fremont to catch the train home.

When I finally got back home to Kensington, the only disturbance I found there was one book fallen from its shelf.

During that time when I'd begun working in San Francisco, I would often come home too exhausted to cook and so would head for the café around the corner from my house—a friendly place, warm and welcoming. I had first met Barbara Mauk there, as we chatted easily from our red-topped stools, sitting at the counter watching the cook make our dinner. We'd become good friends, meeting here after work for several years. She had a little boy, Neil, a shy, tow-headed three-year-old when I first met him; now, three years later, he was learning to read, a curious schoolboy.

I knew they'd gone camping at Point Reyes the weekend before, but where were they now? They should've gotten home well before the earthquake struck.

Then the bleak, devastating news: The park ranger had found them in their van, packed up and ready to leave first thing in the morning. They had slept in the van and had been overcome by charcoal fumes from their not-quite-extinguished broiler.

Neil died. And quite nearly, Barbara.

For three weeks Barbara lay unconscious in the hospital, waking to find her life in devastating ruins.

I watched this amazing woman reach out for the grace to find joy in her life again. After several months, she was able to offer a beautiful ceremony of remembrance for Neil, and then take his ashes to the finest redwood tree she could find and bury him there. It is in Big Basin Park, just north of Santa Cruz. We would go together to visit him, finding solace in that grove of ancient trees.

Barbara eventually left Kensington and her work as a professor's assistant to study homeopathy and aromatherapy and now helps others heal.

Barbara is the embodiment of lovingkindness.

Perhaps the huge storms
of winter are over.

I'll move those strangling
piles of driftwood soon, so
I can get through to walk
on the beach again.

About to retire, after nearly a decade of designing computer software for Southern Pacific, I feel as though I'm about to launch into flight from a cliff, hoping the wings will hold, frantically searching out the best point for leaping, trying to find an updraft.

Who am I now?

Have I really spent my life on the misery of guilt and obligation for being female, bright, curious, alive? I know myself now and hold true, but the world doesn't see me, won't hear me. Why am I put here to know such screaming alienation? How shall I howl it forth? Will *someone* hear me? Or is it only for the Goddess to know me, my voice lost in the sweep of the tide?

I pick up my pen and begin to write.

FOREVER

Reconciliation begins with
telling the stories.

What is it that terrifies me so?

When I went to the DMV to take a driver's test and had handed in my completed form, the clerk started to mark every box wrong, asking, "Did you study for this?"

For a moment I felt entirely in the wrong, intimidated by his certainty, but then when I persuaded him to recheck the answers, he found he was using the wrong key.

This feeling of being completely wrong, like waking up in Mongolia or Timbuktu without a roadmap, makes me wonder if, when I get to heaven, someone on St. Peter's staff will say, "Uh-oh! Computer error; they gave you the wrong script."

I have not bloomed full-bodied and glorious, free and reaching, as I was meant to do. Every time I reached out, I was assaulted, put back in my box: mentors, professors, priests, even friends, all telling me what to think, how to act.

And so *thinking* has become a private thing for me. Having been handed a language, a society, I could barely survive in, I am still asking: *How do I know? What can I really know?*

If I skew the picture a little, can I glimpse a truer vision?

Truth shimmers and slides, a living interaction, not a dead absolute: playful; innocent.

I have stepped outside the boxes, the labels, the archetypes, into the land of no names, no maps, no self.

Yet the ashes still smolder. I want to speak, to be heard, but I am a visionary without craft enough, caught in the poet's song: *Visions stream from burning towers in the graveyard of desire—the spider sings in the wilderness.*

I have been up against a wall of black obsidian. For a while, I felt grounded, like a powerful oak tree, but I am breaking the bonds of guilt, and I am terrified. *Leave behind all baggage, the raft itself. Free-fall through the rapids. Trust.*

The weather turned incredibly windy
and stormy and the power went
out some time after two.

I turned on the propane stove for
heat, then tried to salvage dinner,
which was cooking in the crockpot.

Retired now, I had been looking forward with deep joy to making my last home here, at Camp.

On a pleasant afternoon, sitting out on the deck with one of my daughters, I began describing the little house I'd planned during all those lunch hours at work—a single *great room*, with good acoustics and lots of glass, lots of cedar, set high on slender piers. She abruptly burst into tears when she realized I had in mind a real house, occupying space, needing the road moved, trees cut. She had thought a tiny house, tucked back out of the way, at the farthest edge, invisible.

Then she softly added that one of her brothers had told her he was glad he'd been able to come to see it all again before I ruined it. And that if I'm planning to stay in the cabin while building my place, I'll be in the way. And that I have a right to do this awful thing, but I should realize how they feel, that, after all, it was I who had taught them to love this place.

I feel terrible, shattered, utterly abandoned. I want to leave, to go elsewhere forever. If I'm so much in their way, I should just go.

It rains. The gentle, healing forever rain. The eagle perches high above the cabin.

I go to Langley and talk with Josh at her bookstore. I drive down Sills Road, then Ewing. Such rich country. I go back to the cabin, but I don't go in; I find an FM station and sit in my car in the leafy glade, listening to Scriabin preludes. It is still raining softly.

My dreams shift and slide, crack apart and reassemble into something remote, a thing remembered, like an old photograph. I will never again be at Camp—like my mother was—all summer with my family.

I remember her singing in the kitchen, fussing over the fire in the stove to get the right heat for pancakes; I remember her making blackberry jelly and trekking to Maple Point for clams. She was endlessly patient with her cedar-colored paint samples and her hand-sawn scalloped paneling. I remember her wonder over baby ferns, and maidenhair with their shiny black stems, and how she reveled in the tides and the stars and the great storms that take over everything.

What does *coming home* mean? This is not the vast wonderland of my childhood. The dock and store long rotted, no Princess steaming smartly by to the minute, no little country store; the accordion music from the Brigham's log cabin is a nostalgic, ghostly memory.

If the loss of arena is to lose my voice, the loss of home is to lose my sense of place, to be utterly adrift.

So what now? Perhaps I'll go traveling in my truck, talking to women, drowning in music, dancing, walking in the rain, writing. Perhaps I'll go to high New Mexico where I briefly traveled years ago. I remember being happy there in winter.

I decide to settle in Santa Cruz where Kater has lived all these years. It should be a good place to find my music again after all those intense and focused years of earning my living as a software designer. There are musicians here, writers, a university, bookstores, poetry readings, concerts. I want new friends to love, someone to play music with. I know I need the sea. I hope to be able to bring Tropos to fruition.

I find a small cottage a block from the ocean. There are mountains nearby with redwoods and trails for hiking. And family!

But whoever I was, I am no longer. I'm not finding musicians to play with; the university people are scrabbling after their careers with no time for outsiders; the feminist musicians are all writing pop songs; there's not much classical chamber music happening. There are no resources for a Tropos performance.

I do make some friends, but I'm celibate, not gay, and while that made no difference in Arcata, here it seems to. It turns out to be a long, dwindling time, the windows opaque, all the doors shut tight.

A fter nearly a decade, again it is time to go.

I am sent back to the island by an unexpected hallucination of stead-fast joy—a vision of golden triangles falling, cascade after cascade of living light, like birch leaves let loose, the black, fecund earth hurling back the scent of violets, all shy intensity, opening the skies to forever.

Here, on this island, I have come home. I won't leave again.

I have found a picturesque little house in Langley, built in the forties, with an open-ceilinged great room, farmhouse style, that is just right for my piano, with plenty of room for chamber music.

The house is painted an intense cheerful blue, trimmed in white; there is even a white picket fence. It's all a little too postcard-pretty, so I paint the front door a strong, contrasting dark purple, which fits in with this Victorian village's call for bright colors.

There are plenty of flourishing trees and rhododendrons, and a meadow with rabbits and deer, the occasional eagle. I can easily walk into town to Moonraker Books, the Doghouse Tavern, my bank, the grocery store. I like my neighbors.

I will find friends here.

The day starts easy, overcast, then big fat drops of rain, clearing in the afternoon to become a warm, endless, dreamy day.

I read Rilke's poetry into the soft air.

I am shattering, breaking into a thousand pieces. I never imagined it was so hard to grow old. I must give up everything if I'm to know any serenity. No illusion of Zen-like contentment now, only the hard stripping away of old losses, angers, hopes.

I am lost in it. I can't do it. I can't stop it.

My life has been heavy and harsh and I have been depressed often and long. Yet I have looked up.

This is who I am now.

have been taking astonishing risks—I accept the great and terrible energy of violence. I take in its bone-deep fear, the agony of its pain, the anger, the vitality. I look at it. I wonder at it. I eat it. I wear it. I begin to enjoy it as it becomes soft quilted armor, insulation, comfort—a telegram from my deepest heart.

I pour the rage and fear, the hating and the killing, into the crucible and pour out its miraculous transformation of fierce peace, of fiery-hot, bittersweet compassion, of golden, wide-eyed radiance.

I am being carried by the wind across the sky, I know not where.

The orca is on the move;
I can feel the stirring, the
breathing of wild heart,
wild mind.

I can't do it with words.

I need to howl.

Something shifts deep within me; I am in a place of gathering in.

I have had visions of great fertility. I have put forth a rich world of flowers, a heaven of stars. I have launched baby comets and they have streaked away in brilliance, out of sight for a while, into that mysterious, mythic land that lies east of the sun, west of the moon.

Now they're returning, one by one, full of love and glory, with the smile of the Goddess.

One morning when I went to the piano to start my daily scales, I was stopped by the sound of a cello playing the most beautiful music I could ever imagine—rich, soaring, vibrant music that I had never heard before, not like a Bach sonata, more like Scriabin, one of a kind.

I followed the sound into the next room, to find Kater playing there.

My comet returning?

I could see that the room was filled with enraptured people, but I woke up before I could see who they were, much less what they were doing in my kitchen!

Utterly still.

Soft fog rising under cliffs.

One loon fishing.

What I remember most is the scent of cedar, pungent, clean, sylvan, with a hint of distant cypress—an exalted feeling. We were walking steadily upward, on a slight slope, slipping a little on the silken needles underfoot. I don't know how long we had been walking here, in this shaded place, the hours uncounted, but I could see from the light ahead we were approaching the edge of the forest. The dragon kept close to my side, silent, breathing little puffs of steam into the crisp air.

We emerged onto a grassy headland, to gaze steel-eyed at the next stage of our journey. Before us was a chasm of immense proportions, its far side a blur on the horizon, indistinct in the soft light. This blinding vaporous expanse was filled with a seething icy mist, intensely frigid. The whole landscape was shades of white—pearl, chalk, milky almond, washed-out lavender, luminous ice-blue—all indistinguishable from the sky above it. It was clear to me that I had to cross this formidable abyss.

I shuddered deeply.

I stood for a time petrified like a painting, my staff in one hand, the other resting lightly on the rough head of my companion, whom I called Grandmother, as I breathed deeply down to a sustaining calm. It was only because of her that fear did not beggar my sanity; I trusted her, both deeply as a woman does, and simply, like a child. I would follow her anywhere.

She was small for a dragon, about the size of a wolf and, I would judge, ancient. Her color was deep turquoise, darker around her eyes, and slightly translucent. She seldom spoke, but somehow communicated to me what I needed to know. She loved me.

When she did speak, her voice was smoky and low, whispering: *These are the ice fields of hell. I will give you strength for this journey.*

The clear early morning light was casting long shadows and the ice was turning bright. With a mixture of terror and exhilaration, I stepped forward with the dragon, making the steep descent into that treacherous land.

I quickly lost all sense of direction, all sense of time. Mist rose and swirled, nothing had definition. The freezing fog shrouded every-thing. The soft light seemed to be everywhere, coming from behind the mist and under the ice. Sounds were distorted, direction-less; a complete whiteout.

It was bitterly cold. I had thought the ice would be flat and smooth, but it was not. The terrain was constantly changing. The ice moved and shifted under my feet, yet I could always find sure footing some-where. There were ice dunes, heaps of chunky ice blocks, corrugated slopes, fields of ice gravel. Once I thought I saw a mountain range in the distance, but it vanished—a mirage. The dragon stayed close to me as we moved easily together. It seemed right to be here.

Then we came to a set of wide, steep steps and slowly climbed up them into a palace built entirely of ice. It looked like some sort of natural formation, utterly empty, eerily silent. Trembling lightly, the dragon left me.

I spent a long time, alone now, wandering in that shimmery blue haven, time I don't know how to measure. Eventually I reached a place of deep peace, comforting and rich, and I knew I could trust my ability to finish that terrible journey alone and without fear—I made the steep ascent on the far side of the abyss with no difficulty.

I had crossed the ice fields and I was alive. I emerged into a grove of lovely young trees, sheltered, soft with the green of springtime; their light, sweet scent put me into a healing sleep. Then, refreshed, I walked deeper into the land, following streams, finding waterfalls and grassy meadows. I watched baby birds, played with wolf cubs. Once, I thought I heard the rasping whisper of the dragon passing by, still guarding me.

There were no more trails, no paths, no more seeking; I was confident, serene, and utterly beyond desire. I had merged with the earth and all her beings, the primordial forest, the far blue mountains.

Everywhere felt like deep home.

A gloomy, socked-in morning,
neither wind nor sound.

A single heron fastidiously stalks
down the tide's edge.

It's all quite spare, a sort of
visual haiku.

The island's Unitarian Church choir is going to sing my Spring Round at their Earth Day service. I am delighted that they like it, that I have something to put back into this nurturing community.

I had written it quickly. I'd been working hard on Tropos, thinking about how the women dance and sing when they return from the Land of the Dead. I was alone, heading back home to Walnut Creek from southern Oregon, after a week with Ruth and Jean Mountaingrove. As I was driving my little gray VW south out of the Siskiyous, I sang lustily, working my way through all the rounds I could think of. Suddenly a lilting, flowing rhythm coalesced around the drumbeats of the words *come* and *sing* and *dance*. Yes!

There I was, with no music paper. I pulled over—oblivious to the glorious view of mountains, the redwoods, the beginning of the Sacramento River—and started drawing those careful, parallel staff lines across the only paper I could find—my little notebook meant for travel time and mileage.

I am not an easy composer. I throw in everything I can think of, and then start throwing out all the trite, the sentimental, and the truly awful, hoping for a touch of gold in the residue.

Then something wonderful bursts forth. The women sing:

Come, you people, now praise the good Earth.

Rejoice!

The fields are greening, rivers run wild.

Sing, you little birds, baby beasts, and shiny stars.
Our song is freedom, freedom and liberty.

Oh now dance, yes dance, dance you rocks,
dance you sea, for the springtime has come.

Come, you people, now praise the good Earth ...

(And so on, around again.)

The cosmic dance is a pulse
of coming together
and breaking apart,
of naming and un-naming,
of exclusion and inclusion,
of knowing and un-knowing.

Something gets dredged up that gives me the unholy shudders. Deep, shaking, earthquake shudders. I fold inward, belly-clutching, protective. In deep shock, I sob, I rock. A dark, hard object is being lanced out of me.

If my body feels anguish from being owned, colonized, used, de-formed, then my spirit feels something so far beyond pain that I don't know the name of it. What are the words? How to describe the judgments, pronouncements, ridicule and laughter, being denied my friends, the moral attacks, the lies—all working to destroy my very being? And how to describe the hurt of my acquiescence in order to survive? The abandonment of principle, of integrity? My attempts to adapt to another's structure, values, mind?

Whatever was lanced leaves me devastated, my *self* in rubble. What-ever I thought I was, whatever I thought I'd built, from the moment I first said *I*, seems to be made from lies, innuendo, and half-truths, so mixed up with anything true that I don't know right now what is there.

I am a solitary column of beauty surrounded by old chunks of rock, like some ruin off the coast of Italy.

The dark Goddess, Kali,

the Earth Mother,
who eats the dead,

first gives life.

I remember returning to Berkeley decades after earning my degree there. I was walking through that gorgeous, early spring campus after a concert. The flowers were exquisite—painfully exquisite—innocent, ephemeral. All they do is be what they are, perfectly, without passion or hope. No wonder we who have known the abyss find such solace in flowers. Flowers in the face of death. Flowers for old women. Flowers for bright youth on the cusp of dreams.

I strolled through the music building, remembering when I had a desk there, engrossed in working on old manuscripts. And then feelings I thought I'd gotten well past suddenly erupted again: the power of the professors—the *men's club*—and the way women were never taken seriously. The professors always chose one of the men to mentor, and women who had finished their dissertations were ignored while the men who had yet to complete theirs were recommended for prestigious appointments. The women ended up scrambling unassisted for whatever jobs they could find. One friend ended up accompanying PE classes in the school gym. Another gave up altogether and went back home to finish raising her children.

I know I cannot have the position, the respect—above all, the arena—to play in, to *act* in, that comes after years of establishing one's credentials as teacher, performer, composer. I took a different road. I left academia and went searching for my soul.

Yet for a grotesque moment I felt all that old ambition, the passionate yearning to reach that star.

Wearily, I returned home through all those flowers, tears streaming.

Exhausted from that harsh remembrance, I lay softly asleep in the evening light, dreaming of the Goddess—trusting her, feeling the warmth of her holding me in her arms, knowing she loves me entirely and absolutely.

She raises me to my feet, light and easy; we rest our arms on each other's shoulders, drowning in each other's eyes, in perfect love. Those eyes, so vivid a blue, dark, yet brilliant, have the clarity and luminosity of gems, transparent in their depths, leading into the heart of the universe.

I woke, filled with a gentle joy.

It is simple, elegant, wholly astonishing.

Like the sunrise, this thing we call enlightenment.

Nothing extraordinary, just a gradual diffusion of light as the world becomes clearer and clearer.

The radiance that fills the universe.

After the pain and rage heal, I know I have had a magnificent life.

I am way beyond self, beyond concept, my inner space is huge, passionate. I am an outpouring of this whole astonishing universe.

I've traded the iron convictions of the aging academic for uncertainty and the ecstasy enflaming the ardent heart.

Despite the enormous losses of arena—identity, friends, resources, security, achievement—from abandoning the rich woodlands of academe, I say now how glad I am I took the road I did.

I am free. I can look, I can think. There is no tower to defend.

I am the Goddess Wanderer.

We are vortices of highly organized energy—
the universe experiencing embodied spirit—
energy becoming matter—the *being* that is
constantly arising.

Let us look long and deep into each other's
eyes and slowly smile.

The last time I went with Barbara Mauk to visit Neil's grave we strolled through the redwood grove, talking quietly, circling the huge double tree where her little son's ashes are buried. Neil's tree—one of a kind—is huge and old, blackened, deeply hollowed out by some long-forgotten fire.

Talking and strolling in the redwood grove, we circle the huge double tree that is now Neil's, going through the portal of two young guardian trees into the great charred interior of the mother tree. We caress the satiny new growth that is working its way through the char and admire the gnarly knobs that are growing downward, seeking to root in new earth. It smells strongly of mushroom and dry, moldering twigs and needles, yet somehow a fresh, greenish smell.

We pick our way across the tangled litter of down wood from a recent storm, to sit on an old hulk richly covered with springy moss; we listen to the cry of a little bird, the hammering of a woodpecker, the wet sounds of an unseen waterfall; we seek out the strange magical faces embodied in the great redwood's bark.

Barbara is no longer mourning; she is ready to let Neil's spirit fly free. She won't come here again.

We gaze deeply into each other's eyes, turquoise to azure, for a long, long time.

I wish her a safe journey home.

No breeze stirs;
the anemometer lies still;
a bright-headed eagle
soars easily across the sky.

Julia has died. Julia Gay. I have loved her all my life.

She and I didn't agree about a lot of things when we were growing up. I was often meanspirited when we struggled through adolescence. She wasn't. Her generosity of mind was constant. We often argued, but she never criticized.

I am a little slow. I have eventually realized that she gave me the full, open support that I so much wanted and never got from my mother. She watched with interest when I chose music over physics, stood by my side at my wedding, grieved with me, as only a lifelong friend could, when my mother died. When I became a Catholic, she said it was logical, given the premises; when so many children seemed overwhelming, she babysat. When I turned to the world of computer design, she applauded the renewed exercise of my left brain.

And to think I used to feel sorry for her because her mother didn't know how to tie a hair ribbon correctly, with the knot tucked under in back, or choose acceptable clothes. I was smarter, prettier, more popular, more sophisticated. I don't think much of those ideas now.

Julia died in the early hours of Easter morning in her husband Marko's arms while he tried to breathe for her. When her daughter Nadja called to tell me her mother had died of an overwhelming asthma attack, I was bewildered and couldn't believe her. Julia seemed so vibrant, well-recovered from the ulcerated colitis that had plagued her so much of her life; she and Marko hiked on the beach or up into the hills behind their home nearly every day; she was an activist for civil rights; she was rich in friends.

I got on the next plane to join the family for the memorial. Gradually, I began to realize that what I was feeling was smoldering rage. How could you, Julia? Didn't we have a deal? We'd planned to go traveling together after we retired, to have fun together the way we did when we were ten. Is this how the cosmos rules?

The memorial was simple, a gathering of friends at home in La Jolla. Marko, of course, and their daughters Nadja and Mira, with husbands and grandchildren. Julia's two brothers were too ill to come. There were neighbors and all her friends from The League of Women Voters, but I was the only one who had known her all the years of her life, had known her daughters as babies.

Still, I learned something new: Julia was an internationally known epidemiologist with an entry in *Who's Who*. All she had told me was that she'd done some translating of scientific papers when she lived in Paris. Did her other friends know? They eulogized her lavishly as a dedicated volunteer, a zealous League president.

Nadja, a professional woman herself, was bemused, a little shocked, saying, "I never thought of Mother as a volunteer. Not a volunteer! She was a professional woman!" Mira, subdued and crying, talked softly to the children. Nadja had organized everything, briskly in charge. It was only after all the other guests had left that she let go and we hugged each other for a long time.

On the day Julia died, Marko, remembering his childhood in Slovenia, had slipped down to the Greek Orthodox Church to share in the wonder of the Resurrection service. He told me that an elderly, black-shawled woman had talked to him, telling him that since Julia had died at Easter, she was most assuredly taken straight to heaven and was now and forever with the angels. Marko, softening a little from his scientist's atheism, asked me if I thought this could be possible. We sat talking for an hour or two, the longest conversation we'd ever had, talking about spirit and possibility. He talked about home. And Julia. He was ten years older than her and had thought he would die first, not have to face this emptiness.

Then he said an appalling thing: he'd never told her that he loved her. He asked me if I thought she knew he did. I knew neither of them were demonstrative people, but this was too much! I laughed out loud and reached for his hand and told him all the ways I could remember how she loved him and that she absolutely knew he loved her.

The least I could do for you, my Julia.

I had always thought that some day I would go back to Indiana to find Yolanda and bring her home with me—I'd learned to sight-read; we would make beautiful music together again.

I had sent letters and gifts, but unbeknown to me she couldn't reply; she'd been suffering from prolonged bouts of miserable paranoia, dealing with drugs and hospital visits. Walt had divorced her, taking custody of the children, remarried, lost all contact with us.

There's more. Since childhood, Yolanda had had a heart murmur and now wore a Pacemaker implant. It failed. She died.

I did not know. Alan had learned the whole devastating story quite by chance.

I am covered with fine crazing, the craquelure of an old painting or a fractured windshield of shatterproof glass.

I feel so scattered.

I am here and I am old. And Julia is dead.

This is beauty.

I never knew the hour of Yolanda's passing. No whisper, no desolation, only, one day, that there would be no more music, no more possibility.

I am old and my voice is cracked. I raise my voice, my shattered, scattered voice, in glorious requiem.

And this is beauty.

Surely, even in gauntest senility,
I'll remember at least a shiny
fragment of that raging serenity
of the universe, that glory.

Live fiercely.

Burn with everlasting fire.

Be light.

I sit in the cold, near-solstice sun at dusk, windows open wide to the fresh air, hoping to drive out the damp smell after days of pounding, overlapping storms. I am listening to Jan Garbarek's *Officium*, which begins with *Parce mihi domine*, from the *Officium defunctorum*, a musical setting of the Office of the Dead. The music of Garbarek's saxophone as it blends with the soaring voices of the Hilliard Ensemble fills my heart. It is rich and flowing and intense and spare—angelic. There is a photograph of the jagged and rocky lava fields of Iceland on the disc jacket; it is the *dead* part of the Office of the Dead, looking remarkably like the ice fields from my vision.

We hear music first in linear mode, but afterward, remember the whole of it, the soaring wonder of it. We *know* the way rocks know, pouring forth that knowing in glorious song, in our brief bit of time before again the lava fields, again the silence.

I'm dreaming of Jacob, my intrepid traveler son, riding the rails with the hobos, singing for his dinner in the cowboy towns, fiercely defying the limitations of kidney failure. Garbarek's saxophone is pure fire in the air. It cuts sharp to my core, to a great chunk of fear I didn't know I was holding, that Jacob might die before I see him again.

Six years or sixty, a moment or a millennium, eternity does not distinguish. Understanding this will not soften my heart's pain but it lets me grieve without anger.

I gently release this agony into the music-touched night sky.

There is a place in our galaxy where new stars are forming—the Dark Rift— thousands of light years away.

We are facing that rift now, passing through galactic waves of energy.

It is a wonderful thing to have lived a long life. So much of it drifts into dreamtime. Inadvertent. Scattered. Wheeling from ecstatic heart to scorched soul, from overflowing love to dull duty and bleakest fatigue. And all the ordinary things: pots of aromatic soup, bread baking, earth dug for the garden, sheets flapping in the sun, sweaters mended, stories told, parties given, concerts played, poetry read, graduations and weddings celebrated, earning a living any way I could, making do, giving thanks, learning to listen.

This is the endgame. The last exploration.

It might have been different. How I planned it wasn't even close to as good as what I got. I am not at all what I started out to be.

When I woke up this morning, I was playing a Brahms Intermezzo in my head; not quite the same as playing it on my piano.

My loss of hearing distorts pitch too much for me to take pleasure in acoustic—heard—music, so I must rely on memory and imagination; a different part of the brain.

It's as though a large chunk, a whole compartment of my brain is lost; a soul-nourishing part, something unique.

It is just gone.

Yet I remember the way the ecstasy feels.

Lacking an arena, I have come to live on this island. I have come home.

Here, there is no need to speak—my songs unfold only to my inner ear. There is sound enough in the archaic dance of the black fir trees, the slow deep beat of the great blue heron heading home, the delicate flutter of unexpected snow.

I am nourished by the constant mountains and the constancy of changing tides.

Meditation falters into nothingness for I am already everywhere. Ambition dissolves, anger has no meaning. Fleeting bitterness, the acid taste of failure, hold no power; they are but gossamer remembrance.

What I've found is the hard-won wisdom of the ancients, the love that takes no return.

Beautiful, beautiful day.

High, brilliant, snowy mountains;
that solitary loon again.

I like to watch the *sun-stand-still.*

The setting sun moves from high on Double Bluff at summer's solstice to a place just south of the entire range of the Olympics at winter's solstice, where it scarcely moves for several days, then swings back, picking up speed faster and faster until the equinox, then it slows back down, scarcely moving again back at summer's solstice.

This apparent shifting of the setting sun from north to south and back again is the result of our orbit—we're the ones moving, not the sun.

And I like to watch the moon disappear for a day or two before presenting itself as a tiny sliver, then a crescent, then gibbous, then full—riding as high in the winter sky as the sun does in summer.

The earth turning, turning: sunset, moonset, starset too.

Three great, irregular circles interlocking in a shimmering, shifting, cosmic dance, writing it all onto the tides—bringing all kinds of joy to my dear mathematical heart.

For one cataclysmic, incandescent moment I understood everything.

Now, for the telling of it, words are incomplete and unsatisfactory, clumsy as broken rocks, the vision evanescent and eely with laughter at my presumption.

September 10, 2001. Fall is just a hint, silent and mysterious. The summer of the grandchildren—that I had anticipated so eagerly in May—is now a bright blur. The hot earthy joys of those months slip away into memory.

The dogwood's leaves are brittle, a bit rusty; all the trees look dark and heavy, almost ready to shed their leaves. The air tastes fresher, with hints of fog and wood smoke. The sea shows its dark side, the kelp and seaweed are heavier, the tides later, scatterings of sandpipers and geese on the move.

The sun has set well south of Double Bluff for some time now; it is almost the equinox. Subtly shifting toward lavender, slightly iridescent, the light has less blaze; everything is easier to look at.

Every fall I feel this way, but I don't know the name for it. Soft, slightly sad, dreamy, like nostalgia, but without ache for the past. Rather a gathering in, waiting for the turning of the night.

It is a time for music and weaving, a time for wood fires and hot soup, for poetry and stories; a time for dreams, and a time to remember the dead. An archaic feeling. There is the hint of something lost. Where didn't I pay attention? Whom didn't I love? What did I miss on the road not taken?

This feeling, this *opposite-of-nostalgia*, presages a dark edge. If the coming equinox is a soft gray opal, then the solstice is inky onyx. We know what's on the way—the dark, bleak time.

The balsamic
moon is frightened
to lose her light.

And then the World Trade Center came crashing down. After disbelief comes horror, then somber sorrow. All crowded out by nausea and fear as I listen to the voices clamoring for blood, for revenge, for more violence. Oh let us stop the violence, let us stop it right now! We need to heal the earth, not destroy her.

How is it we have become the most destructive nation on earth? Does it come from the great conflict between gold-seekers and liberty-seekers? From the potent mix of our feeling entitled to both power and righteousness? Is it bound up with the struggle over slavery? The genocide of the indigenous peoples? The brutal struggle to settle—to subdue—half a continent?

It's not enough we destroy all the indigenous people we can and the great herds of animals and flocks of birds; we destroy the forests and prairies, we put aquifers and fragile tundra at risk—even the very air. Then we go on to destroy whole cities by fire, by nuclear explosion; we ruin small countries, destroy governments. We are thorough.

Somewhere there are people who want to do this terrible destruction to *us*. There are men who willingly and faithfully give their lives for it. The whole thing is horrendous beyond description and we all have a part in it.

Suddenly I am prostrate on the floor, praying as profoundly as I can for the souls of these valiant men whom we so fiercely hate.

Then I thank the Sacred Creator, the Great Holy Mystery, for the healers among us, the light seekers, the loving brave ones. I will bring radiance into my house. I will pray for peace with each passing flight of birds.

Dread floods my soul.

We are having a War.

Again.

Another protracted inconclusive carnage. I am in agony over what this means. The killing. The blanket hatred. The eager embrace of government control; full-out fascism. The planet gets destroyed while the guys with robot eyes grab their money, even as they turn to stone.

Terrified, I want to simplify. Dump everything. Go find a cave. Live in profound solitude.

Awareness sifting like soft fog in the black light just before dawn, dull, thudding with a deep soul pain, thick with the need to weep.

September 11, 2002.

Grief merges with grief, a seamless roar, not from the flames and smoke, but from the breaking of hearts, the splintering of families.

The horror of New York overlaid with Sarajevo's. Horror upon horror: Viet Nam, Laos, Cambodia; Hiroshima and Nagasaki; Dresden; Coventry; and dimly, Guernica.

Then endemic despair.

I feel it all. I am the Mother, the Mystical Body, the Universe.

Lying exhausted in the somber half-light, I struggle to get myself into place—here, now—to set my edges.

Wind! Wind! Wind!

So many different rhythms—a great patchwork
sky throwing bits of brilliantly lit, frothy clouds
around with sodden blackish ones, flashing bits
of bright blue;

the traveling sea, crashing its heaving waves
in that peculiarly irregular yet steady rhythm,
all the while sinking, being sucked up the inlet
in the relentless tidal gravity;

madly dancing bushes and bare branches,
with the whole hillside alive with old, noble firs
and cedars stiffly swaying.

Here on the deck, the driftwood sculpture
shudders, the boards creak, while some phantom
sets the rocking chair off—rapid, crazy.

Tremors speed through the house,
but the electricity holds.

I am an old wolf howling at the moon. I am so tired. I am faltering. I have lost my nerve.

Sometimes I howl in agony for want of a deep intimacy, the shape and touch of another, for want of falling softly into the gentle embrace of someone who cares who I am, who lets me care about them, let's me love their scent, their texture, who offers vulnerability for vulnerability, dream for dream.

Someone who says, "What did you do this morning?" Or, "Look at the light, how lavender it looks this time of year!" Or, "Listen to this, what a splendid poem!" Or, "Here, I'll do that." "Shall I light a fire? It's getting cold tonight." "Would you like some wine?" "Are you hungry? Let's have some soup." "Are you getting sleepy?" "Would you like to play a little music?"

Then I remember I am a contemplative. I do not turn toward partner or friend; I am open like a crystal to whatever light the universe sheds upon me.

Every moment is an epiphany. I move through my day in an ecstasy that is as comfortable as homespun, ordinary as oatmeal. I feel everything—the doom that flows through us like slow, black blood, even as I'm lifted high into the white-hot blaze of glory.

I've been contemplating the vagaries and subtleties of Beethoven's Opus 109 for a long time now. This requires, like a meditation, intense focus and a loving attitude. His exploration of the key of E is sweeping, thorough. He sets out a broad, interlacing palette, drives deep into its essential energy, exposing its succinct essence. Thoughtful and reflective at first, he becomes assertive, urgent. Then—oh, brilliant—a theme and variations, so lovely, turned this way and that, seen from different angles of light, broken apart wide to the extremes of space; then, oh so gently, caressed into a final joyful remembrance.

Wabi-sabi: the esthetic of austere, elegant simplicity, embodying respect for the old, the broken, the lost, the flawed, slightly smoky with melancholy and nostalgia, yet intimate and serene.

Nothing lasts.

Nothing is finished.

Nothing is perfect.

This evening tears pour down my face, a waterfall of emotion I don't know how to name; a catharsis of joy mixed with wonder and gratitude: I am here, alive, aware.

It started with the dancing.

The New York City Ballet aired a retrospective of recent new works. And how they did dance! Going to the limit of ways to be a body, creating a fluid space, a living, changing, collective sculpture, drawing me into their evocation of loneliness or intimacy or playfulness or tragedy, opening in me an intense inner space, a bright awareness, an unpredictable and unprotectable vulnerability.

Suddenly, those gifted dancers—light and traveling—are dancing Tropos, with its haunting dissonances, its deep visceral rhythms, its searing lyric moments. How Tropos moves me! How Tropos has shaped my being!

Wide open, I was entirely susceptible to the avalanche of emotion I experienced when next I watched the emergence of the three- and four-thousand-year-old bodies that had been found in Western China. A man, two women, and a child; Caucasian, well-preserved; bodies, not artifacts.

I felt close to them, especially one of the women, how she must have lived, watching her animals graze, calling to her children, cooking dinner, weaving the lovely plaid woolen garments worn in her grave. And how she had so carefully combed her hair, a soft light reddish color, still neat in two smooth braids after all those centuries.

Again, I found my face wet with tears. This ability to know history—time—seems to work on our emotions just as art does.

I finished the evening finding solace in the rich archaic music of the movie *Elizabeth*, watching that lovely young girl face down the brutal truths of her life and turn herself into the heroic Virgin Queen, the regal embodiment of her country.

Art—exploring our collective spiritual embodiment—acts as catalyst for the whole community. We experience each other through jazz, poetry, skyscrapers, Gregorian chant, graffiti, ancient Greek temples, hymns, murals, novels, the great classical works, the sculpture in the plazas, the cathedrals. This is how we remember who we are.

The sun is traveling fast now that
we are almost at the equinox.

It is already past Mount Constance.

It's difficult to realize that it's really
moving at the same speed as it
does at the solstice—*sun-stand-still*.

After Barbara's little son died, she moved away to a tiny town in northern California's Trinity Alps where she became an aromatherapist and perfumier.

I hold in my hand a small vial of scent she built for me; it is called Peace and Tranquility of the Will.

I let one drop fall to my wrist, then inhale deeply.

The aroma of trees, dark conifers, surrounds me, fills me. There is also a lightness—a penetration of clarity and equilibrium—along with a deep grounding of earth scent, moist and loamy.

Soft pearl-gray dawn, luminous.

A mockingbird begins its first spring song—a few tentative notes, some experimental variations, then soaring into its full kaleidoscopic patterns— sounds equivalent to luminous.

This rich time of transcendence, of understanding the unbreakable unity of body and spirit, is a time of sensuous lucid dreaming.

I have crossed those fierce ice fields and rested in the uncharted forests of the farther shore. I have been visited by wolf cubs.

I have experienced the state of no-concept, which stays with me now as a ground to all that I think and experience. Concept and no-concept coexist, as yin to yang; as the space and the reverse space of the turning spiral; as the silence and the sound of music.

I am both woman and Goddess, here now and eternal, fragmented and whole—utterly still at the center of a node, fierce light shimmering and vibrating all around.

Remembering when I was about to cross those ice fields, I am dreaming at the edge of the precipice. I understand now that this journey is dangerous and must be prepared for extensively. And so I give myself into the care of the Old One who will prepare me with her strong hands and loving eyes to go to that place beyond desire.

First she massages me, deep, sensual, relaxing. I feel the tension stripped out of every muscle. Her voice strips away all self-doubt as she repeats how strong, courageous, beautiful, loving, I am. This takes a long time. I come to feel whole—nothing scattered—rich.

I move as though the air were thick. I drift, without gravity. Dreamy. Well, it *is* a dream.

The Old One's helpers are small, delicate women, who now prepare my body. I am bathed in jasmine. The scent finds its way deep within, purifying, cleansing. The first wave of erotic feeling breaks over me. These little climaxes are marvelous, there are no barriers as they rip through me—delicious. I am laughing. The women are touching me, gentle hands everywhere, smoothing, increasing my awareness. They rub in aromatic gels, and the soft air becomes thick and heady with the scent of roses and night-scented stock.

My senses are becoming vastly heightened. It feels intense just to *be*. The women have sloughed off all impurities. My hair has become translucent and smooth as flax, thick, and perfectly straight. The gel has tightened my skin, smoothing it down to a baby firmness; I am silken and alive. They are stroking my face, kissing my ears, my eyes, the tender places between my toes, the soles of my feet. They are stroking my vulva, my soft, soft pubes, my eager clit—I am out of my mind with joy.

They are circling, dancing their fingers, finally reaching my breasts, which soften into great pools of feeling, building, building. Everywhere, I am brightly sensitive; I am crackling like wildfire. They are strewing me with herbs and wildflowers, then a great shower of tiny ice crystals. Just as I explode, the Old One looks deep into my eyes from her smoldering turquoise ones and gives me a deep soul kiss.

From the cool darkness it feels as though eons have passed. My awareness returns slowly, languorously. There is a casement window, soft air drifting over sparkling, filmy, white curtains. I eat a peach, sun-drenched, warm, dripping with rich, sweet, red juice.

The women come to dress me. The air feels like spring, light and slightly warm. I stand straight and tall, ageless, vibrant. They drape a glowing sapphire robe around me, then start to do my hair. Strand by strand they weave in long shining strips—some to match my hair, some like fire—until my hair is a cascade of light reaching to my knees. They have woven in strands of crystal and silver shot. Light is dancing and shooting everywhere.

Now I am standing in a flowery meadow. This time is special, it is completely for me. Everyone is admiring me; I am like a perfect rose. Then I see a perfect red rose between the teeth of a startlingly handsome man, naked save for his richly embroidered, elegant black vest. Smiling, he gives me the rose, then fades away.

There is more of this sort of thing, I can't remember all of it. The meadow has become a float; I am drifting past all the admiring people. By the time I reach the split-rail fence, I am ebullient. Four gorgeous men are leaning on the fence, beautiful in their bronzed nakedness and their huge, oversized ten-gallon hats.

As I drift past, they turn toward me and, as one, with perfect timing, flip their flags to full, pointed alert. They laugh, in homage. As I drift on, they look down in amazement to see their penises and crotches bedecked with clusters of Sweet William and pinks in all their rich, rosy hues.

And on, through mists and swirling colors. I find myself unable to tell up from down, here from there—not exactly disembodied but without boundaries.

All the first part of this dream was only a preparation. Now, I am completely open. The Old One is with me, but I can't see her. I can't see anything but color, light, darkness, mist—there are no shapes or edges.

There is no preamble here, I am instantly fully aware of all my senses. I groan out, "Enough, I am full," but the Old One answers, "It is just beginning."

The women have surrounded me, stroking me with delicate sapphire feathers, a touch I can scarcely feel, transporting me to new levels of awareness, tiny dots of intensity everywhere. They blow their honey-flavored breath over me in hot little bursts. They have put little balls of aromatic oil in my vagina, and whenever I move or cry out, one of the balls bursts, flooding the night with nicotiana, and jasmine—once, the sharp, lifting tang of lemon thyme.

The Old One strokes my feet—the toes, the soles. She strokes faster, deeper. If there is any barrier left, she heals it. All my strength is in my feet; then it lifts, fills, pours out; my skin is nothing, I am pouring everywhere, up, beyond myself. I am flourishing like a tree. I am a shooting star. I am becoming ... becoming: *everything.*

I am quieter now, my spirit full. I must have passed out. How long was I like that? It feels like forever. The intensity still fills me. "Hush," the Old One says, "it's not the time for remembering, yet."

I am distracted by high, faint sounds. The music has begun, like far-off Tibetan bells ebbing and flowing to a rhythm all their own. I am in the loving place, the giving place—the giving that is the sharing of love that never stops, never comes or goes.

The Old One gives me something to drink in a small silver bowl. Whatever I felt before, I now feel inside of me: breath, heart, tissue, bone, all the places within. This goes on for a long, long time. It is beyond ecstasy, beyond all feeling.

Because I am so diffuse, so *everywhere*, it is only gradually that I become aware that I am *loving*. In the deepest place within me, a pure gem, an unconsumable essence, burns hot sapphire—a deep, fiery blue tinged with flashes of darkest red.

My heart?

My beyond-self me?

I am radiant with it, hot, emanating every kind of epiphany: cascades of tiny flowers and green grasses, myriads of them, pouring from my fingertips, the ends of my hair, my toes, all shining brightly. And myriads, myriads of stars from my mouth and womb, endless flights of birds, schools of silvery, tiny fishes, laughing babies, bits of song, showers of crystal raindrops.

The music is rising in me, becoming me. The sound of a deep, reverberating gong rocks me on its echoes; its humming never stops, sliding from one harmonic to another, like laughter, like a mountain stream. The bells pool and ebb. Then another sound, a dry rasping crackle, the wind of a firestorm, rising, filling, roaring with awe—the dragon passing by.

"Now drink this," the Old One's voice comes to me softly. Her arms fold around me, holding me. "This is for remembering." "Yes," I say, "I want that."

And so it all starts again, from the beginning; I remember all of it. It is so vivid I can't tell if I am remembering it or if I am living it. Three times I drink from her silver cup, remembering ... remembering ... Whatever I was, I am no more. I am now light. I am love.

At last I say, "I am enough."

"Yes," she says. "Now drink from the cup of Nepenthe, the cup of forgetting. Your body will always remember, as will your heart and that part of your spirit that is beyond consciousness; but to go on living you must veil that intensity, although you will always know it is there. You will know only serenity, for you have been perfectly filled and perfectly loved."

I won't have this dream again—it is a farewell.

The sun darts into my hanging
crystal and dances emerald
and sapphire;

I remember the sea, alight
from within, swinging gently
in its earthen bowl.

Great beating wings lift me up
and I am in an ecstasy of sky.

A strange thing, this dying.

I watch the body of the Pope, the Papa, being carried from his home in the Vatican Palace all about the great plaza of St. Peter's and into the basilica. Tens of thousands are chanting the Miserere—*Have mercy on me, O God*—and the Litany of Saints, calling upon all the saints of heaven to pray for this man. Thousands of miles away, I join in, remembering another day in Florence, in the Piazza Santa Croce, during Lent, a smaller crowd, calling down these same prayers for all of us on earth.

Even in death, this man, John Paul, doesn't seem at all diminished. We are told that although he is dead, he is still speaking to us. And so it seems. There he is, borne aloft by his dear householders, dressed in robes of highest ceremony, vestments chosen for the death of a Pope—white for purity and faith, bright red for compassion, the heart and fire of the Holy Spirit. His head is almost obscured by the great double-horned bishop's miter, his thin, slippered feet, somehow poignantly unaligned, pointing outward.

And his spirit soars. It seems to fill the square. It pours out over the hills, the ocean. I feel it passing—a soft, urgent movement, a gentle chinook—as he joins the universe.

A great sea of people has come to do him homage and to pray for his eternity. All the scarlet cardinals, the violet monsignors, the metropolitans, the monks, nuns, bishops and archbishops, deacons, laity, and, no doubt, angels and seraphim, had we eyes to see. Race, nationality, gender, blend together in a single cry of "Pray for him."

I have felt badly judged by the men who are in charge of this religion: *They* are in the image of God and I am not. We are asked to call upon Father and Lord. The Goddess is not and will not be named. Every time God is mentioned, women must make a little jolt of adjustment, similar to that adjustment we make when we hear the pronoun *he* or a word such as *mankind* that is used for all of us. Prayers and liturgy need continuous translation: Father to Mother, Brother to Sister, Lord to Friend. No wonder we feel more fully grounded or nourished or comforted in the arms of the Goddess.

Pray for him.

A drowning wave of humility engulfs me; today I see them only as souls like mine, beyond classification or gender.

Sometimes when I forget to be afraid of people and their judgments, I see in them a great tenderness and vulnerability and desire, and for a moment their faces are as luminous as angels.

With a great clattering of wings—a distinctive and unforgettable sound, a lot like old-fashioned heavy wooden Venetian blinds falling downstairs—two shadowy, winged beings made their presence known to me. Somber. Immense. Powerful.

It was at the culmination of an intense weekend retreat of purification and renewal taking place at an old farmhouse in the lush meadow that used to be the Deer Lagoon estuary here on Whidbey Island. I was standing before about twenty women—my turn to tell my story.

Abruptly, without words, the two beings flooded my senses with understanding. They were, I knew, bodhisattvas, protecting me and those I love, keeping us from despair. In awe, I returned their love with deep gratitude.

Then, quietly, I asked, "But why are there two of you?" In a laughing rumble, they replied, "We knew that if there were only one of us, you wouldn't believe it!"

And then they were silently gone as the music of Leon Fleisher began playing into the airy, sunlit room.

Days lengthening, tree buds swelling, crows nesting, water gurgling to the sea, as the earth hurtles toward the equinox, pulsing into a crazy hope, a wild joy.

Once more, whales!

Once more, birdsong!

Once more, roses!

I'd lived here at *Maris Stella* for just a few months when I had a gallbladder infection that sent me to the hospital during a severe, prolonged freeze two days before Christmas. The last thing I remembered was rumbling over my rocky path on a stretcher, looking up to see two eagles, perched low on a looming pine tree; they were watching me intently in that severe way eagles have and I knew the bodhisattvas had come to protect me; they wouldn't let me die, even though I felt ready enough.

Hospitals, surgeons, nurses, drugs.

Then rehab.

Get me out of here!

I don't know who I am any more.

This place is full of some seriously incapacitated people: they are old. I don't even know where this place is—limbo somewhere. I can see one gull, three crows, an airplane, low, skimming past what looks like a fortress, but it's too small, and floodlights on a well-kept soccer field. There's not even traffic to watch here.

I don't like it here. It's all too clean, too Prozac. We're not allowed to sound depressed or talk about dying. We're all facsimiles—resigned, mute.

I come to realize that I'm in the old place in the woods north of Seattle that was used for recovering tuberculosis patients when I was a child; the medieval fortress turns out to be the power plant.

I need to focus on *something*: sudoku, Italian, calculus.

This is hard. It's noisy, the meals come *way* too early. But there's no point in feeling bad, so I don't. Instead, I watch the fir trees—such tall, dark, beautiful beings—swaying gently in the soft breeze.

Sometimes people think I am strong, but I am not. Home now after rehab, I am deeply shaken. I feel *old*. I have to be careful— I might fall, I might need help. I'm supposed to wear an alert button. My kids want someone to check on me.

I had to face that I could have died and I'm okay with that, but I feel tired, utterly flat. There is no tomorrow.

I haven't felt like roadkill before—two-dimensional, empty.

I want to feel differently from the way I do, but I know I must revel in the feelings I *do* have.

There is a heron on the post: duly noted; brants go by, flying low: duly noted. It's a windy, dull day, clouds like a mattress. I feel heavy. It's hard to walk. I was hurting all night. Duly noted.

I am intensely grateful for the bodhisattvas.

I will learn to live again.

I seek the vastness of certain solitude, living quietly now, paying attention.

I think a lot about dying. I thought I would die in that place, but I didn't.

I think a lot about those who have died: Yolanda, Julia, Alan, David's hours-old baby Gabriel, little Neil, Victoria, Ken.

When Ken died, it was six weeks until his wife Elizabeth was able to tell me; no announcement, no ceremony. I mourned him in my own way. He is always there, the fourth corner of my first family, his presence a smoky haze drifting through my stories.

Remembering Ken

I swim in ancient Lethe
    soak up the way of Death
        inward-turning eye
            opaque with dreaming

gather down the darkness
    gritty clinging fog
        no comfort there

smooth silent alabaster-flashing onyx
    no ordinary waters these
        receiving ice to ice
        ordinary and all

all seek the sweet forgetting
    let loose the grave cloak of despair
        bitter smell of wet wool drowning
            mute, stripped, release old stony tears

dusky shadows ragged, drifting
    ghostly echoes confound the senses
        tear apart the loom of time

then Mother's faint silvery voice
    calling over the years
        Kenny ... Peggy ... time to come home

come back dear brother
    you shining boy!
        I'll remember you ... I'll remember

where eagle hunts and orca sounds
    where the small rain makes all fresh
        where wild starlight meets fecund beach
        we'll play again as children
            remembering ... remembering ...

Hey Mom, I'm here, with my Goddess self.
I love you. I hope you're happy.

I know you didn't mean to hurt me,
you wanted me to be wonderful.

Can you see me now?
Do you love my children?
Aren't they beautiful?

I'm sorry you couldn't share my life.

You left me so alone.

Waterfalls fascinate me—what marvels of sight joined to sound. Water gives us so many beauties—snowy mountains, glaciers, fog, great heaving seas, delicate rainbows. But I especially like waterfalls. They are so rich, full of sound—the delicate splashing of the baby ones to the massive gut-filled roar of the mightiest. Their color shifts from the blackest green to rainbow-studded foam. They just keep coming and coming, pouring afresh, bringing life to our earth, to us.

They fill me with hope.

When I lived in Langley, I saved lots of photographs of waterfalls and made them into a dream board, a bulletin board I hung near my bed. I added a few other things—lots of small mandalas, a photo of the view of the Arcata marsh in the mist, a Boulet painting of the Goddess, the Dalai Lama reading a book while working out on a treadmill in full robes (both inspiration and joke), a few quotations, an Alaskan glacier.

Since moving here to *Maris Stella,* I haven't needed it in the same way. It's like an old scrapbook now, an artifact, nostalgic. Perhaps I'll hang it in the study for remembrance.

The sea is flat, metallic, calm,
after days of heaving turmoil.

Oh, how I love living on this
watery planet!

Sometimes this place, my home here at the beach, however beautiful, seems pallid, a thin presence in what was once a teeming wilderness of immense abundance. I've seen photographs, I've imagined what once was.

Those tiny native oysters, the Olympias, covered every bit of shore where the tide wasn't too swift, richly flourishing from San Francisco Bay down the coast as far as Mexico and north into British Columbia. They were the Sound's filtration system, siphoning off every impurity, keeping the wilderness pristine. Baby salmon loved this gentle nursery, returning from the sea as great fish, glutting the wide rivers as they came home to spawn.

I've eaten these oysters once or twice with my mother—I think it was on the Oregon trip; they are a delight, rich and slightly smoky, firm in texture. The newer, big ones seem lacking in flavor and are a trifle spongy and slimy, needing lemon or a pungent sauce to save them.

They were too wonderful, these keepers of the wilderness. Seeing them as icons of success, the newly rich miners of the Gold Rush wanted them for their lavish celebratory feasts.

They ate them all.

The vernal equinox is Monday
and I am so glad of it.

What a winter it has been.
I am ready for a new burst of life.

I've already been visited by crows,
a robin, a chipmunk, gulls and terns,
of course, and a long skein of geese.

The scientist says that by definition, information belongs to neither mind nor body, although, traveling between the two realms, it touches both, thereby allowing us to transcend the mind-body split of the basic assumptions of simple force and response that have been ingrained in our consciousness since the sixteenth and seventeenth centuries. The language of information theory—relatedness, cooperation, interdependence, synergy—helps us break out of our old patterns of thought. We are beginning to conceptualize a different model of the universe and our place in it.

No whitecaps, no sails;
thick sodden April rain
sends home the eagle's
white flash.

When the Plains Indian tribes were being exterminated by our government or captured and rounded up and corralled into reservations, their prophets and religious leaders were visited almost simultaneously by a vision—or promise or prophecy—that their land and their people and the animals they depended upon would yet one day be restored, that even in the depths of their misery—especially in the depths of their misery—they could take solace in the knowledge that the buffalo would roam the plains again and that their people would once more be strong and free, as would the wild land itself.

When the Mayans, those great cosmographers, said the first age would end in 2012, did they know that meant our consciousness would shift?

The poet says *it's a kind of music, like making a fire by slamming two rocks together—hitting words together with rhythm and sound quality and fierce playfulness. It's an immense conversation of the soul, driven by justice and healing, transforming experiences that could potentially destroy a people, a family, a person, to experiences that build connection and community.*

I have somehow taken inside of me the whole planet for healing. The tectonic rage of the Mother for the earth and all of her people fuels my mind's and soul's cry, *We must all live in a new way!*

The lessons of otherness are harsh and fast now. It is clear that Western Civilization is crashing. This great masculine construct— dominant, hierarchic, brilliant, destructive—is dissolving into the sea, a shimmering white carapace, all vitality washed away. We're on the cusp of an upheaval, a catastrophic shift of consciousness such as we haven't seen in thousands of years.

There is terrible fear.

Violence, despair, and general anomie throw up dust clouds that obscure what's happening. Huge amounts of energy are shifting everything in our culture from the familiar—separation and objec- tivity—to the realization of unity and interbeing. And it's happening faster than lightning.

This is not the archaic, undifferentiated, oceanic awareness of our earliest beginnings; it is the full and simultaneous experience of sepa- ration together with indivisible unity.

While men have been creating our dominant culture, women have been doing it differently. Arising from a profoundly different gender experience, women's consciousness is more intuitive and cooperative, closer to emotional mind, closer to collective instincts.

But as a necessity for survival as the suppressed gender, women have also developed an understanding of men's consciousness. This leads to a deep, holistic consciousness, one of unity and interbeing, not just with each other but with all life, with the planet itself.

We know we're all interconnected. We know enough about quantum physics and force fields to be astonished and bemused. We know that time is not what we thought it was, that we are living in eternity right now. We know that matter is energy, and so is spirit. We know that being is constantly arising, the universe seeking consciousness.

All that is eternal, all-knowing, full of infinite possibility, permeates all that is created, finite, time-bound and particular—infinity seeking duality.

It is the Goddess experiencing other.

Consciousness is shifting toward this paradox—the unity of interbeing at the same time as the separation of objectivity.

The change will be profound. It will be obvious that the most broken and hurt among us need the most compassion. Food and shelter will be shared. The hatred and insanity of our world will dissolve, war will seem like nightmare's enigmatic joke. Our world will flourish, not as a colony to be exploited, but as what it is—our *home.*

We will make new myths, sing new songs. We will all be watchers of the glory, and we will be there, drawing the water, hauling the wood, cooking dinner, rocking the baby.

What a chill at the enormity of it! We are—by our consciousness, our *thinking*—creating evolution.

We are remembering who we are.

Vernal Equinox.

Light from the east silently
suffuses the sky, its radiance
renewing the life of the earth.

It is the glory time.

It is easy to feel close to the Goddess in the dark, mist-shrouded, tall forests of the rainy country; easy in the rich web of the ocean's rhythms. But let my soul remember that the Goddess is there holding us in the deep pits of our lives, the mystical dark nights, the scrabbling at the edge of the abyss. The Goddess is there in our sooty cities, in the dingy streets, and all the earth below. And in all the gloomy weather—the dull, the gray, the so-so—nothing at all sublime.

As a contemplative, I have watched every aspect of the ordinary, seen how magical everything is, how luminous it is to *be*. No matter what we do, the Goddess is there. Our evasions, our sentimentality, our rationalizations, all our gritty pettiness do not diminish Her. She is with us always, always—when we're washing dishes, picking strawberries, driving trucks; and when we're weak and clouded, arguing, stealing, running stop signs, talking with our mouths full.

It's the heart that asks the question,
the poet says, not the furious mind.

It sees and knows everything.
It hears the gnashing even as
it hears the blessing.

The door to the mind should
only open from the heart.

It is a time for contemplation, a time to write, a time to read poetry, a time for endless hours sitting on the deck watching the tides and the birds and the westering sun.

It is not in the meditation or the practice, the ritual, the theology—it is every morning receiving from the Great Mystery and giving back the glory—coming into harmony and beauty; it is the mystery of the pipe of peace, the mystery of nothingness, the mystery of the communion at mass, the mystery of Orpheus; it is the three little children, high on that great rock in Rio, dancing the sun up at the end of the film *Black Orpheus*; it is the singing of angels and seraphim; it is the great Alleluia.

And then proceeding through the day as best you can with loving-kindness in all that you do, giving and receiving.

John sent me an astonishing book of poetry. I thought I was too old for something so new and galvanic keeping me up half the night. The poet writes like an osprey fishing—one gaspingly accurate dive, then a little crunching of the bones and it's all over. A sonnet!

I don't know what it means, or even if it's any good. It doesn't *mean* anything, there's no time for that. Just instant, blazing understanding at the heart of the paradox that is both profound alienation and forever love.

John is the poet—how gloriously grateful I am for his love and his expression of it. He says he doesn't believe in God, that the world just *is*. Fine with me. God is pure Being.

So what have we said?

The thing is, John loves the *is* with an ardor any monk could envy.

Fill us at daybreak
with Your love
that all our days
we may sing
for joy.

My time here is nearly done.

My whole life has been lived in deep autumn and I finally understand that I will not come into full flower in this lifetime.

What a strange odyssey it has been, wandering among the tombs of men.

I am becoming one of the Grandmothers. Old. Ancient. Iconic. Time is losing its meaning.

I thought dying would be a violent separation of body from spirit, an exhaustion of the temporal. Instead, dying now, I feel the unity as strongly as ever, but *everything* is shadowy, quietly dissolving.

I am becoming ephemeral.

At early light, gently awakening to greet the day, I softly whisper …

Not today.

It is both gratitude and petition.

O Grandmother, O Ancient One, who will dream your dreams, know your wisdom, see your visions, when all the people work, making, breaking, sorting everything into boxes, sending it all off to oblivion?

When the philosophers are done, and the diggers, the users, the restless chemists, and the sanitation engineers; when the historians are done making their centuries and categories, I will remember your wholeness, Mother. I will tear down the fine, tight web of divisions and distinctions, pour out the rancid brew of *other/them*, burn away the hatreds and greeds, and look and look and look until your ancient loving rises like smoke-mist in the morning.

I dreamt that I was becoming a tree,
like that archaic statue of a young
woman fleeing Apollo.

I become leafy, twining, vital, green,
full of light, deeply rooted, without
gender—entirely tree.

I seem to be in some sort of Zen graveyard for lost musicians. I am flooded with music that won't let go—the E minor Mozart sonata that I used to play with that exquisite and fearless violinist, Yolanda.

The sonata is intense, somber, long-lined and lean; it carries you and carries you and carries you, then gently settles you in the center of your heart's grief.

Yolanda is long dead. I can't play anymore.

Old age is so very, very strange. I grieve. I howl. I empty all my tears, blindsided; the sonata: ashes.

The tragic melody lingers gently—half-heard, bittersweet—like the slightly acrid scent of dissipating smoke.

Art:

messy,
uninhibited,
ecstatic.

A howl.

The amazing thing about the Chihuly installation at the Kew Gardens in London is how it galvanizes the heart into hot creativity and hope. Abruptly, one realizes that our beloved green and blue planet, so torn between issues of the natural world and the civilized one, still has the possibility to be transformed and healed.

Chihuly calls his installation *Mille Fiori,* a thousand flowers. His working style is organic—no molded clones here. He works with the forces of gravity and centrifuge, blowing, lifting, whirling, dancing, dazzling, occasionally caressing or snipping, to create entirely unique beings, his *fiori.* They are vibrant and strange, sparkling or drawing the light inward, shy or brazen. An obdurate, scattered substance is transformed by immense heat into a malleable, luminous, slippery substance that keeps its new shape when cooled, while becoming frangible and highly luminous—the sand has trapped the sun.

The *fiori* sit well in their new green world, near or beneath the great glass houses of Kew. Bulbs and orbs of intense blue enhance the shimmer of the bright green that shelters them. Club-like stalks of deep dark red stand aloof, yet compelling, an irregular cluster shadowed by a leafy overhang. The agave, dull turquoise and sharp-pointed, seems even richer and sharper for the presence of its apparent flowering of thin white and crystal shafts—oddly appropriate offspring. Two great *trees,* bounteous clusters of balloon-like gourds, dipping and writhing in their rich reds and golds, stranger than a monkey-puzzle tree, as magnificent as any magnolia, stand guardians-at-the-gate. If these beings seem bizarre, imagine the first traveler who ever saw an orchid, a bird-of-paradise, a saguaro cactus.

That natural quality of *myriadicity,* or bounty, is well explored, especially where there is water. Hundreds of orbs set free on the pond, with a little rowboat drifting under a tree, filled to overflowing with bright watching beings. And lilies! Great exotic reticulated lily pads, appearing to belong more to Chihuly than nature, all tucked around with smaller golden gleaming glass ones. Everything, glass or green, seems to say, "Look! Look!"

The complementarity between organic and artificial, between natural and civilized, goes both ways. Chihuly's vision draws the organic into the artifact, so that all those luminous bright-colored beings look entirely appropriate amidst the lush greenery. But that greenery is not entirely natural either. We are not in the depths of the rain forest jungle; this is not wilderness. These are botanical gardens, sophisticated collections of exotica displayed in one of the world's most sophisticated cities. These plants are not only unique in themselves, some are among the last few specimens of their species, cultivated, cherished. They are nurtured apart from nature, under the high glass roofs that concentrate the sunlight and warmth needed for their survival. They are fed, watered, cared for; they are named.

This interplay, this commentary on art and nature, affected me deeply, drawing forth feelings of warmth and delight. I felt as though, at least for a little while, these ancient, conflicting forces of wilderness and civilization that so split apart our lives were sharing a harmony of spirit and healing. Thus beauty into hope.

I experienced a tremendous surge of creative energy, throwing me out of that regular box of normality into a crazy, crystalline place where anything can happen. Music was rising up within me.

It is fiercely invigorating to have my mind taken over by these large abstract sounds that have a life of their own. They take form as sonic clusters. I am hearing a sound garden, luminous as Chihuly's glass— clusters of sound, great dramatic explosions, glorious surges, big patches like red stalks rising vertical as smoke, birdsong shimmering high over eerie glassy planes of sound, a high mist settling. Playful beings chatter to each other, then transform into a loose cluster of somber statements, undercurrents rise, then settle, the harp passing through, stately, slow. Planes of shimmer, lakes of tone, with intermittent punctuation, the perspective constantly shifting, and the heart-stopping truth in the magnificent voice of the great Taiko drum. Arching over all this, a soprano, clear as glass, singing fragments of joy in all their chromatic variation: *Gloria! Gloria! Gloria!*

This work of *garden* music is completely abstract, yet it evokes the organic. There is no melody, no so-called *meaning*. Its only form or structure is its own necessity. It is a garden of sonic events, my own *mille fiori,* that simply bursts forth into its own glorious ephemeral being.

It's a soft rainy night after a biting, windy storm. At music's end I close my eyes and remember the sea after such a storm: turgid, metallic, swift.

Fiery, molten glass from the furnace
cools, shatters.

Fiery, molten glass from the furnace
cools, becomes art.

Tropos sits on a shelf in my study, a compact artifact of my life. Three large folders that fit easily into a single box, page after page of careful, tiny black notes inscribed on oversized manuscript paper, fourteen staves to a page. No one writes like that anymore; it's all done by computer now.

Tropos has defined my life, bringing me great riches of spirit. The story of a flawed love, it resonates deeply within me—haunting, powerful, a liturgy—the urn of life shattering in deep silence, the long dance through dreams and visions into the forever time.

No one else has ever heard that final, luminous music of reconciliation—it has yet to be performed. It is a last ecstasy, heard only in my inner ear.

High upon a rock, with visions of decaying civilizations swirling about him, stands Orastel, old and ghostly, clutching arrows and mace—his emblems of power. Yurdah berates him for forgetting that he is the poet, then invites him to come down to her, to rejoin humankind.

(Yurdah)

Woe to the poet
who blinds his inner eye
and stops his beating heart!

Woe to the poet
who smashes down his harp,
mute as freezing rock!

Woe! Woe to the poet!

Pride has spawned a kingdom.
Greed has built a monument.
Power has named your gods.

Woe! Woe to the poet!

(Orastel)

It is the time when visions stream from
burning towers in the graveyard of desire,
the spider sings in the wilderness,

dark valleys yearn for rain,
the voices of dead children
rise softly in the wind.

My cities crumble, silent stone
beneath the hungry sea,
my laws have scarred the living earth,
my arrows pierce the sky.

My songs grow old,
my heart turns gray.

Let Tropos turn again!

(Yurdah)

Come, dear exile, come home with me!
Leave your death, leave your fear,
let sorrow go!
We cannot mourn our ancient loss:
proud beauty, honor, guilt.

Now leave the blood-drenched hearth
for liberty's shining web
and join in human bond!

(Orastel)

No more exile, I'll come with thee,
leave my death, leave my fear,
let sorrow go.

(Together)

Put down all judgments!
Put down all divisions!
Put down all fiery pride!

Put down dominion,
the masks of madness
and all the acts of war!

Put down, put down all war!

Alan died Monday morning. The door closes gently.

I am remembering ... remembering ...

An ardent outpouring of love to our children: Whatever he did not or could not do, however closed off he was, he always loved you deep in his heart.

You never knew him when he was young and heedless—the brilliant, insouciant, poet—a baby transforms everything. We both fell in love with them, of course—deeply, unconditionally—but Alan was inexorably changed the day he became a father, entering the difficult territory of responsibility and conscientiousness—a hard, demanding land, however full of awe.

Still I love him, despite everything. No, because of everything. I will love him forever.

I hope he is happy, that he is free.

I know he loves.

Pentecost—

Come, Holy Spirit,
fill the hearts of Thy faithful
and kindle in them the fire
of Thy love.

The ospreys are back!

Last chance!
The eleventh hour!

Or not.

It might be only the tenth.
It might be the last day.

No one knows.
No one *can* know.

So I live on the edge,
serene and alert.

Slowly, so gently, like the sifting of twilight in these northern latitudes, that fierce embodiment of spirit, of heart and mind, that has been my life for more than ninety years, is becoming diffuse, easing away from time. Having courage too small to name, I find it speck by speck through long gray days, until clear, dry age etches radiance into the forever dust.

I don't know how to die. I can't imagine not being here, in this place, on this planet. I can't imagine not breathing the cool air, not feeling the freshening wind. I can't imagine the tide hauling out heavily in the early light, the great majestic, eternal, seaward mountains laying their jagged silhouette against the lightening sky, and I am not there—no sundown, no sea lifting its light from pale pink to mauve to lavender.

There is only one time like today. Oh, how I sink my teeth into its richness, taste its color, drink its air, pour remembrance into those beloved mountains that are floating now high over the pristine clouds rising out of Hood Canal.

How could there not be another and another of this? How could I possibly not be there? Be *here*?

Who will know what I know? Love what I love?

So many different concepts of the afterlife: Will there be redemption? Glory? Judgment? Horror? Simple erasure? What will happen to me? Will I *be* only in someone's memory?

Still, my imagination slams shut. Well, so be it.

At the crossroads of time and eternity, the story never ends; every moment, being arises, always changing, yet eternal. My spirit will live forever.

Sometimes I lie awake, waiting for first light, and wonder at the exquisite purity of all the rhythms pulsing and flowing through this world of time. How shall I experience music—that quintessential temporal ecstasy—in eternity?

Will I know it all at once? A totality of the sublime?

Is eternity perhaps like music remembered, where the end is known from the beginning, that remembrance illuminating its resolution? Perhaps it's like life itself—risky, flawed, dangerous, but whose outcome is certain, safe, and perfect.

The endgame is nearly played,
the future opaque.

All I can see is love.

I had a dream, a lucid dream, half awake. It takes many words to describe it, many pictures to visualize it, but it was almost instantaneous, pure intuition. I simply knew these things were so.

Now it is haunting me; I woke to it again this morning.

It is many hundreds of years in the future. I can see the earth—the blue watery planet—then North America, zooming in to the countryside we now call Arizona and New Mexico. The world is filled with loose clusters of people, living lightly on the land. They are happy, they love the children and the elders, not just their own families, but all the children, all the elders. They are well-cared for. People are connected and help with each other's difficulties before they get out of balance.

They are beautiful, too. You can see in their faces the high cheekbones and bronze coloring of their First Nation ancestors, or the tawny colors of Asia, ebony from Africa, blended into a new people.

Sometimes a child is born with blue eyes and ivory skin or bright hair. Then the people marvel and the elders remind them of the old myths that tell of a strange race of violent people who rampaged across the country all those centuries ago, pouring across the eastern sea from the far world.

They made a great merchant empire with an insatiable need to consume everything in sight. They said they wanted liberty, but only for themselves. They killed the First People and brought others here into slavery. They said that their god was love, but they worshiped power and they lived in constant bone-deep fear of becoming powerless. They neglected their spirits and eventually self-destructed. It was a tragic time.

Then the people circle around the children and hold each other a little closer. They begin to sing.

It is not so much that I saw or heard this, I just came to understand it.

Gradually I was filled with a warmth and well-being that eased the tension of all those war-mongering years, that can only be called grace. I felt so light and lifted up into joy. And I knew without words needing to be spoken that all shall be well.

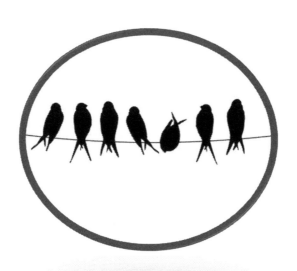

Acknowledgement

I am dying. Dissolving. Becoming effervescent. It is intensely physical. The flesh is burning off, transformed by the acid in the ashes of time. Strange. Painful.

And I am grateful.

I have learned from everyone I have ever known. In particular, all those mentioned or alluded to in this book, especially my beloved children and grandchildren:

Kater, Mar, Thomas, Sarah, John, Jacob, Michael, David, Makaela, Moriah, Zoe, Ryann, Caroline, Cassia, Anna, Caelan, Cassidy, Amy, Nick, Nico, Liam.

Special gratitude to John, the poet-editor, my son, who dared to play with my stories and fragments, who understood my themes, intertwining my use of reverberation, and who kept reminding me how to remember.

Remember. Remember who you are.

— Urashan, *The Goddess Wanderer*

Afterword

On more than one occasion while I was talking with Urashan about her writing and development of this book, she'd sometimes almost offhandedly say that "it was hard to survive in a world that was trying to kill me." This stunned me the first time I heard her say it—I thought she was being hyperbolic, dramatic—but after reading *The Sacred Ordinary* (many times over as I edited it and reworked it with her), I began to understand what she meant. This is the story of a remarkable and passionate woman whose heart and intelligence were overshadowed, overlooked, devalued, turned away, dismissed, disappeared, even annihilated, yet who found a way of *sacred being* in a world that glorifies *doing*, especially the doings of men.

This is memoir only to the extent that Urashan's life serves as scaffolding for exploring the meaning of living the sacred ordinary as a strong-minded woman and non-sequestered contemplative born on the threshold of the Great Depression, coming of age during World War II, raising eight children through the politically tumultuous and war-torn '60s and '70s, reinventing herself after the end of her marriage and again after retirement, and coming to terms with what it meant to be a brilliant woman of the twentieth century, profoundly handicapped by culturally accepted, unacknowledged misogyny. This book is all at once history, feminist treatise, and self-exploration as model for the evolution of the human spirit, all interwoven with sense of place, of identity, of memory, of wonder, of glory, of universality, of interconnectedness....

Scholars, poets, seekers, and lovers of language will find much to explore here, so full of intertwining and reverberating references, allusions, themes, and symbols is *The Sacred Ordinary*—bird, flower, tree, star, mountain, water, music, beauty, death, light, darkness, loss and redemption, purpose and non-purpose, sense of place and exploration—and of course, always remembering, remembering; not the stories so much as their meanings, their emotional essences. This is Urashan's life as archetypes: the Musician, the Mathematician, the Astronomer, the Scientist, the Poet, the Thinker, the Lover, the Philosopher, the Contemplative, the Wonderer, the Explorer, the Mother ... the Goddess Wanderer.

As representation of everywoman (everyone), of *all-spirit*, of the *IS*, "Goddess" is, in Urashan's words, "shorthand for an idea, the essence that matches or rather envelopes the particular environs one finds oneself in. The Goddess in *The Sacred Ordinary* is both the creator and the creation of the being that wells up in every instant from everything we know; *She* is manifester and manifestation of the universe—all at once embodying and being embodied by. The Goddess as simultaneously the self and the whole of the universe."

This is not a linear or a complete history of Urashan's lived life. Rather, it is a *sense* of her experience of life—an exploration of constant becoming and of learning how to *be* in a world that is more inclined to notice and reward the actor, the *doer*. It is about what she thought and felt and discovered along the way, so there are stories about her childhood and her parents and grandparents and ancestors, and there are stories about what happened in her life as an adult woman as she made her way through the twentieth century (and on into the twenty-first as an elder woman). But these stories are emblematic, integral to the book as a whole, alchemically inter-leaved with excerpts from Urashan's mythic dance opera, *Tropos: The Sacred Wheel,* with prayer-like reverences for the native peoples who came before her, and with her haiku-esque poetry and epigraphic contemplations. These "fragments" (as Urashan and I came to refer to them) present in turn an arc of their own, grounding the book in the here and now as if told in person over the course of the dark, cold season: mid-December, just before the winter solstice, to the time of the flourishing of new life just after the spring equinox and the descent of the Holy Spirit at Pentecost.

Taken as a whole, *The Sacred Ordinary* is indeed, as Urashan describes it, a "story-poem, using stories the way poets use words," and like the best poems, it echoes backward and forward and all over—contrapuntally—so that everywhere one *touches* the book it shimmers like a spiderweb across the pages. Or, held like a conch shell to one's ear, all the lines resonate back in one great song: *the spider singing in the wilderness.*

This is Urashan's magnum opus, an artistic culmination, her grand finale of all she has expressed—poetic canon, introspective chronicle, enigmatic pilgrimage—life as sojourn, the body as ashram. I suspect readers will feel by book's end as though they too have "sunk deep into the long-ago time looking for the source of our roots and found the long unnoticed living sap of the ancients still vital in us, deep and rich as womb-blood."

— John Schelling Pollock, Editor

Notes

*"If I remembered what I had forgotten
I would have remembered it."*

— Urashan

It would take another full-length book to exhaustively connect the network of allusions, overtones, and reverberating references in *The Sacred Ordinary*. These Notes, then, are a rudimentary beginning toward that end, to give readers a sense of how nearly everywhere one touches this book it shimmers across the pages, connecting themes and subjects in a tapestry of connotative and associative nuance. Because footnotes would interrupt the rhythm and flow of the carefully organized text, these Notes are placed here at the end for readers and scholars who may wish to further explore and expand their understanding of the "reverberations" that resonate throughout the book.

1   The dictionary defines "ordinary" as "the regular or customary condition or course of things, of a kind to be expected in the normal order of events: routine, commonplace, usual." In Roman Catholic and other Western Christian liturgies, "the ordinary" refers to the part of the Eucharist or canonical hours that is reasonably constant without regard to the date on which the service is performed—everyday prayers that don't change with the day or season. The *ordinary* is contrasted with the *proper*, which is that part of these liturgies that varies according to the date, either representing an observance within the liturgical year or of a particular saint or significant event; and to the *common*, which contains those parts that are common to an entire category of saints, such as apostles or martyrs.

3   *The Cloude of Unknowyng* is a series of letters written in the 14th century by an unknown monk to his disciple instructing him or her in the way of divine union. The text is a spiritual guide on contemplative prayer, the underlying message being that the way to know God is to abandon consideration of God's particular activities and attributes, and be courageous enough to surrender one's mind and ego to the realm of *unknowing*: "When I say 'darkness,' I mean a privation of knowing, just as whatever you do not know or have forgotten is dark to you, because you do not see it with your spiritual eyes. For this reason, that which is between you and your God is termed not a cloud of the air but a cloud of unknowing. If you are to experience God or to see God at all, insofar as it is possible here, it must always be in this cloud." [en.wikipedia.org/wiki/The_Cloud_of_Unknowing]

7   God spoke: In the beginning was the Word, and the Word was with God, and the Word was God. (John 1:1)

11 The way of a contemplative is a lifelong exaltation with *God* in prayer and worship, turning from all else that could make the commune less unswerving. Contemplatives are concerned less with themselves and more with Godliness and all those whom *God* loves. Contemplatives are called to make their whole lives a prayer in solitude and silence and community.

13 "Ave Maris Stella" ("Hail Star of the Sea") is a Marian hymn used at Vespers (sundown prayer service) from about the eighth century. It was a particular favorite of those chanting it as part of the Divine Office (the Liturgy of the Hours) in the Middle Ages: the portal to heaven, forever pure. "Our Lady, Star of the Sea" is an ancient title for the Virgin Mary. The Goddess Venus is also referred to as "The Star of the Sea," as is her namesake, the planet Venus. This is where Urashan's name for her beach house arises. (See also page 19.)

19 Stan Pocock added to Seattle architect Paul Kirk's original design using leftover cedar from racing shells from his family's shop. [pocock.com/about/history]

20 "Sea rote" is the sound of waves breaking on the shore.

20 "Slouching toward Zen" alludes to both Joan Didion's collection of essays, *Slouching Towards Bethlehem,* about her experiences in 1960s California; and W. B. Yeats's 1919 poem "The Second

Coming," the ending line from which Didion took her book title. [poetryfoundation.org/poems/43290/the-second-coming]

24 See page 154 in the book about the family move from the University of Notre Dame, Indiana to St. Mary's College, California.

24 One of the guiding principles of the Catholic Worker movement is hospitality toward those on the margin of society, based on the principles of social justice, communitarianism, and personalism.

24 Advent, Latin for "coming," commences on the fourth Sunday before Christmas. It is a time of expectant waiting and preparation for the celebration of the Nativity of Jesus.

27 "Death is the mother of beauty" is a line from the Wallace Stevens poem, "Sunday Morning." [poetryfoundation.org/poetrymagazine/poems/13261/sunday-morning]

29 Emily Dickinson was a mid-19th century American poet who lived much of her life in isolation. To make the abstract tangible, to define meaning without confining it, to inhabit a house that never became a prison, Dickinson created in her writing a distinctively elliptical language for expressing what was possible but not yet realized. [poetryfoundation.org/poets/emily-dickinson]

33 Pierre Teilhard de Chardin, a French idealist philosopher and Jesuit priest, trained as a paleontologist and geologist and took part in the discovery of the Peking Man. He conceived the vitalist idea of the Omega Point (a maximum level of complexity and consciousness toward which he believed the universe was evolving), and further developed the concept of a noosphere (sphere of reason). In *The Mass on the World* he writes: "In the beginning was Power, intelligent, loving, energizing. In the beginning was the Word, supremely capable of mastering and molding whatever might come into being in the world of matter. In the beginning there were not coldness and darkness; there was Fire. Far from light emerging gradually out of the womb of our darkness, it is the Light, existing before all else was made which, patiently, surely, eliminates our darkness."

33 The storyteller is Charles Williams, author of *The Greater Trumps* to which this fragment refers. The Tarot pack, the ancestor of all playing cards, was conceived of as having magical properties, and the most

powerful of all the cards were the Magic Arcana or Greater Trumps, twenty-two symbolic pictures whose mysteries have been interpreted and reinterpreted over the centuries by occultists, religious thinkers, psychoanalysts, and literary anthropologists. In the universe evoked by Charles Williams, he explores the meaning of all cosmic processes, both microscopic and macroscopic, which he calls "The Dance of Life." Selfish and egocentric use of these archetypal images is shown to be disastrous while their proper use reveals love at the core of the dance. [gutenberg.net.au/ebooks06/0608881h.html]

33 The lama is Tenzin Wangyal Rinpoche, a teacher of the Bon Tibetan religious tradition, and author of *Tibetan Sound Healing: Guided Practices to Activate the Power of Sacred Sound.*

35 John Donne was an English poet and cleric in the Church of England. He is considered the pre-eminent representative of the metaphysical poets. *Devotions Upon Emergent Occasions,* from which this poem is excerpted, is a series of "devotions" he wrote when he was seriously ill in the winter of 1623.

45 *Mirlbindee* is both the stick and the art of telling stories in the sand. [thewest.com.au/news/goldfields/beauty-balance-in-cultural-blend-ng-ya-338223]

49 The Snohomish were amalgamated with The Tulalip Tribes with the Snoqualmie, Skykomish, Skagit, Suiattle, Samish, Stillaguamish, and other allied tribes and bands signatory to the 1855 Treaty of Point Elliott. [tulaliptribes-nsn.gov/whoweare/aboutus]

53 "The Great War" refers to World War I.

56 *Popular Mechanics* is a magazine of popular science and technology; founded in 1902, it features automotive, home, outdoor, electronics, science, do-it-yourself, and technology topics.

61 Chautauqua was an adult education movement in the United States, highly popular in the late 19th and early 20th centuries. Chautauqua assemblies expanded and spread throughout rural America until the mid-1920s. The Chautauqua brought entertainment and culture for the whole community, with speakers, teachers, musicians, showmen, preachers, and specialists of the day.

61 "The Great War" refers to World War I.

62 Zeno's paradoxes are a set of philosophical problems generally thought to have been devised by Greek philosopher Zeno of Elea to support Parmenides' doctrine that contrary to the evidence of one's senses, the belief in plurality and change is mistaken, and in particular that motion is nothing but an illusion. [plato.stanford.edu/entries/paradox-zeno]

62 The Yangtze is the longest river in Asia, the third-longest in the world, and the longest in the world to flow entirely within one country. It rises in the northern part of the Tibetan Plateau and flows 3,900 miles to the East China Sea.

62 Cloisonné is an ancient technique for decorating metalwork objects by adding compartments (cloisons) to the metal object by soldering or affixing silver or gold wires or thin strips placed on their edges. These remain visible in the finished piece, separating the different compartments of the enamel or inlays, which are often of several colors. Cloisonné enamel objects are worked on with enamel powder made into a paste, which is then fired in a kiln.

67 Reims Cathedral (Notre-Dame de Reims) is a Roman Catholic cathedral in Reims, France. Construction on the cathedral began in 1211; it was dedicated to the Virgin Mary and is famous for being the traditional location for the coronation of the kings of France.

67 Nike, in Greek mythology, is the Winged Goddess of Victory.

70 The Shriners, established in 1870, are known by the red fezzes that members wear. They describe themselves as a fraternity based on fun, fellowship, and the Masonic principles of brotherly love, relief, and truth.

73 *Elsie Dinsmore* is a children's book series written by Martha Finley between 1867 and 1905. The books deal with a constant moral conflict between Christian principles and familial loyalty.

73 *The Hardy Boys*, Frank and Joe Hardy, are fictional characters who appear in several mystery series for children and teens. The series revolves around the teenagers acting as amateur sleuths, solving

cases that stumped their adult counterparts. The characters were created by American writer Edward Stratemeyer and the books were written by several ghostwriters under the collective pseudonym Franklin W. Dixon.

73   *Ramona* is an 1884 American novel written by Helen Hunt Jackson. Set in Southern California after the Mexican–American War, it portrays the life of a mixed-race Irish–Native American orphan girl, who suffers racial discrimination and hardship. Originally serialized in the Christian Union on a weekly basis, the novel became immensely popular.

73   Sir Walter Scott was a Scottish historical novelist, poet, playwright and historian. Many of his works remain classics of both English-language literature and of Scottish literature. Famous titles include *Ivanhoe, Rob Roy, Old Mortality, The Lady of the Lake, Waverley, The Heart of Midlothian,* and *The Bride of Lammermoor.*

73   Gaius Julius Caesar was a populist Roman dictator, politician, and military general who played a critical role in the events that led to the demise of the Roman Republic and the rise of the Roman Empire. He was also a historian and wrote Latin prose.

73   Publius Vergilius Maro (Virgil) was an ancient Roman poet of the Augustan period.

74   Douglas Fairbanks was an American actor, screenwriter, director, and producer. He was best known for his swashbuckling roles in silent films, including *The Thief of Bagdad, Robin Hood,* and *The Mark of Zorro.*

74   *The Thief of Bagdad* is a 1924 American silent swashbuckler film. Freely adapted from One Thousand and One Nights, it tells the story of a thief who falls in love with the daughter of the Caliph of Baghdad.

76   "There Was a Little Girl" was written in 1904 by Henry Wadsworth Longfellow. [bartleby.com/360/1/120.html]

79   "Oley Oley Olsen free" probably started out as "all-ee, all-ee, outs in free," a call from the person who was "it" letting those hiding know it was safe to come back to base in the children's game of *Hide-and-*

seek. The phrase is also used to coordinate hidden players in the game *Kick-the-can,* where a group of children hide within a given radius and a seeker is left to guard a can filled with rocks. [appalachianhistory.net/2017/06/ollie-ollie-in-come-free.html]

80   See page 19 entry about the Pocock family.

80   See page 13 entry about "Maris Stella."

82   *Scamper* is referred back to here on page 249 of the book.

86   "The War" refers to World War II.

95   See page 19 entry about the Pocock cedar racing shells.

102 The seaside City of Langley is located about 7.5 miles northeast from Maxwelton on the opposite side of Whidbey Island.

114 The first Chetzemoka (ferry), named after the former chief of the S'Klallam Tribe, worked the Port Townsend-Edmonds route from 1938 to 1947 and then moved to the Mukilteo-Columbia Beach (Clinton, Whidbey Island) route. The name "honors the natives of the region and their seafaring skills and traditions." [evergreenfleet.com/mvchetzemoka.html]

124 *Hansel and Gretel* (German: *Hänsel und Gretel*) is an opera by nineteenth-century composer Engelbert Humperdinck, who described it as a *Märchenoper* (fairy-tale opera). It is much admired for its folk music-inspired themes, one of the most famous being the "Abendsegen" ("Evening Benediction") from Act 2 which "that ethereal lullaby of guardian angels" refers to.

129 According to the *Sunset Western Garden Book* "madrona" is used north of the Siskiyou Mountains and "madrone" is used south of the Siskiyou Mountains (see page 282 entry). In British Columbia, the trees are simply known by the name "arbutus." All refer to the same tree, *arbutus menziesii*, native to the Pacific Northwest and Northern California regions. [ppo.puyallup.wsu.edu/pmr/names]

131 See page 129 entry about "madrona" vs "madrone."

132 "The War" refers to World War II.

132 Victory Gardens, also called War Gardens, were vegetable, fruit, and herb gardens planted at private residences and public parks in the United States, United Kingdom, Canada, Australia, and Germany during World War I and World War II.

141 "The War" refers to World War II.

143 Sappho was born probably in 620 B.C. An Archaic Greek poet from the island of Lesbos, Sappho is known for her lyric poetry, written to be sung while accompanied by a lyre. In ancient times, Sappho was widely regarded as one of the greatest lyric poets of her time and was referred to by Plato as "the Tenth Muse." Most of Sappho's poetry is now lost—what has survived is mostly only in fragmentary form. Her work expressed love for men and women while also paying homage to the deities of the times. [poetryfoundation.org/poets/sappho]

146 "The War" refers to World War II.

156 Pope John XXIII was elected to the Papal throne on October 28, 1958. This was shortly before his 77th birthday. Many thought of him as a placeholder or caretaker pope. They had hopes he would have a short reign and would just keep the Catholic Church afloat during a tumultuous time in the world. Much to everyone's surprise, he called for an ecumenical council, known as The Second Vatican Council, that would transform the Catholic Church into what we know it as today. The main aim of Vatican II, which began on October 11, 1962, was to improve the relationship between the Church and the modern world. Pope John XXIII wanted to "throw open the windows of the church and let the fresh air of the spirit blow through." [shalem.org/2019/10/11/wisdom-of-the-good-pope-pope-john-xxiii]

159 The first three verses of "Where Have All the Flowers Gone?" were written by Pete Seeger in 1955; additional verses were added in 1960 by Joe Hickerson. Its rhetorical "where?" and meditation on death place the song in the *ubi sunt* tradition. (Sometimes interpreted to indicate nostalgia, the *ubi sunt* motif is actually a meditation on mortality and life's transience. Taken from the Latin *Ubi sunt qui ante nos fuerunt?,* meaning "Where are those who were before us?") [wordsinthebucket.com/where-have-all-the-flowers-gone]

161 Russell Means' article in the December 1980 Mother Jones issue originated as a controversial speech given at the Black Hills International Survival Gathering on the Pine Ridge Reservation in July 1980. Notably, Means reluctantly allowed his speech to be

transcribed to text, saying, "I detest writing. The process itself epitomizes the European concept of 'legitimate thinking'—what is written has an importance that is denied the spoken. My culture, the Lakota culture, has an oral tradition, so I ordinarily reject writing. It is one of the white world's ways of destroying the cultures of non-European peoples, the imposing of an abstraction over the spoken relationship of a people." [motherjones.com/politics/2012/10/russell-means-mother-jones-interview-1980]

167   Julian of Norwich (1342-c.1416) is known almost only through her book, *The Revelations of Divine Love,* based on a series of sixteen visions she received on the 8th of May 1373. Julian's actual name is unknown—it is taken from St. Julian's Church in Norwich where she lived as an anchoress (a spiritual counselor) for most of her life. Considering that, at the time, the citizens of Norwich suffered from plague and poverty, as well as a famine, she must have counseled a lot of people in pain. Yet, her writings are suffused with hope and trust in God's goodness. Her message remains one of hope and trust in God, whose compassionate love is always given to us. In this all-gracious God there can be no element of wrath: "Wrath, all that is contrary to peace and love—is in us and not in God. The gift of God's spirit is to slake our wrath in the power of his merciful and compassionate love." She did not perceive God as blaming or judging us, but as enfolding us in love, referring to Jesus as our Mother. [juliancentre.org/about/about-julian-of-norwich.html]

171   The war referred to here is the Vietnam War.

173   Much has been written about the myth of Orpheus and Eurydice (from *Eurudike*, "she whose justice extends widely"). It completes Virgil's classic (29 BC) poem, *Georgics* (see page 73 entry on Virgil); Ovid's version of the myth, in his *Metamorphoses*, was published a few decades later and employs a different poetic emphasis and purpose. Other ancient writers treated Orpheus's visit to the under-world more negatively; in Plato's *Symposium*, for instance, he sees Orpheus as a coward—his love was not *true* (he was not willing to die for it)—so he makes Eurydice only an apparition and has the women murder him. Urashan's *Tropos; The Sacred Wheel* is a reimagining of this myth from a woman's perspective.

174   Describing the myth of *Tropos: The Sacred Wheel*, Urashan writes: "A myth is difficult to describe adequately, for it is, like a poem, its own best utterance. ... The myth of Tropos is at once archaic and of

the future; it is a simple myth: love, death, and return. It is the love of the woman to the poet and their relationship to the Goddess and the great wheel of the universe." Excerpts from this mythic dance opera are woven seamlessly into the fabric of *The Sacred Ordinary* so that the Goddess, the Poet (Orastel), Everywoman (Yurdah), are integral to both. (For other references to Tropos, see pp 190-191, 218-219, 225, 235-236, 240, 246-247, 269, 282, 318, 370-371, 392.) [For more information about Tropos and inquiries about producing it, please contact: info@marisstellapress.com]

174 Haida and Kwakiutl peoples have lived in Northwest America since at least 200 BC. Many of them migrated southward to the Pacific coast of what is now the United States and some of them continued on until they reached Central and South America; the Haida and Kwakiutl people of present day share a close genetic link to the Chumash people of California, the Yaghan people of Tierra Del Fuego in Chile, and the Cayapa (Chachi) people of Ecuador. Defined by deep cuts into the wood and a minimal use of paint reserved for emphasis purposes, Kwakiutl art is similar to other indigenous Northwest coast art that employs *punning* or *kenning*—a style that fills visual voids with independent figures and motifs. Haida art— distinguished by its use of black slate material called argillite—often depicts mythical spirits, animals, family crests, replicas of totem poles, bentwood boxes, and canoes. [britannica.com/topic/Kwakiutl and spiritsofthewestcoast.com/collections/haida-art]

183 Professor Norman Springer and his wife, fellow English professor Mary Springer, were Alan's colleagues at St Mary's College, and family friends.

185 Leon Fleisher is an American pianist and conductor. Fleisher lost the use of his right hand in 1964 due to a condition that was eventually diagnosed as focal dystonia. In the 1990s, Fleisher was able to ameliorate his focal dystonia symptoms after experimental botox injections to the point where he could play with both hands again. In 2004, Vanguard Classics released Leon Fleisher's first "two-handed" recording since the 1960s, entitled "Two Hands."

186 Foulweather Bluff is almost exactly west of Maxwelton Beach across Puget Sound on the north end of the Kitsap Penninsula and on the east side of the entrance to Hood Canal.

187 Yonnondio is an Iroquois term; the sense of the word is "lament for the lost" and refers to Walt Whitman's poem of the same name, first published in 1887 and later annexed to the 1892 edition of *Leaves of Grass*: "Yonnondio! Yonnondio! ... A muffled sonorous sound, a wailing word is borne / through the air for a moment, / Then blank and gone and still, and utterly lost."

198 See page 20 entry about "sea rote."

201 The Pleiades, also known as the Seven Sisters, are a star cluster in the constellation of Taurus (which also happens to be Urashan's astrological birth sign). It is among the nearest star clusters to Earth and is the cluster most obvious to the naked eye in the night sky. The name of the Pleiades comes from Ancient Greek, "to sail," because the season of navigation began with their heliacal rising. [arxiv.org/ftp/arxiv/papers/0810/0810.1592.pdf]

212 Point Reyes is a prominent cape located in Marin County approximately 50 miles northwest of Walnut Creek (where Urashan was living at this time).

213 Attributed to the Ojibwe. (See also page 274 entry.)

219 See page 13 entry about "Ave Maris Stella."

225 The Hupa and the Yurok are two North American Indian tribes of the coastal mountains in Northern California between what is now Eureka and Crescent city.

233 *A Wizard of Earthsea* explores young protagonist Ged's process of learning to cope with power and coming to terms with death. The novel carries Taoist themes about the fundamental balance in the universe that is closely tied to the idea that language and names have power to affect the material world and alter this balance. (Le Guin, Ursula K. *A Wizard of Earthsea*. Boston: Parnassus Press, 1968.)

238 See page 3 entry about *The Cloude of Unknowyng*.

239 The Trappist monk may refer to Paul Quenon, author of *In Praise of the Useless Life*. (Quenon, Paul. *In Praise of the Useless Life*. Notre Dame: Ave Maria Press, 2018.)

246 The Green Party is a left-wing, anti-war federation of state political parties in the United States that promotes "green" politics focused on ecology, nonviolence, social justice, grassroots democracy, gender equality, LGBTQ rights, and anti-racism. [gp.org]

249 The Loma Prieta earthquake, responsible for 63 deaths and 3,757 injuries, occurred on California's Central Coast on October 17, 1989 at 5:04 p.m. The magnitude 6.9 seism was centered in The Forest of Nisene Marks State Park approximately 10 miles northeast of Santa Cruz on a section of the San Andreas Fault System and was named for the nearby Loma Prieta Peak in the Santa Cruz Mountains.

249 *Scamper* was the small boat Urashan's father chartered when she was a child; described in detail on pages 82-83 of the book.

252 See page 249 entry about the Loma Prieta earthquake.

254 See page 212 entry about Point Reyes.

267 Josh Hauser is the owner of Moonraker Books in Langley on Whidbey Island, and Urashan's long-time friend since she opened her bookstore in 1972. (See also page 271 in the book.)

267 See page 102 entry about the City of Langley.

271 See page 102 entry about the City of Langley.

271 Moonraker Books, in Langley on Whidbey Island, is owned and operated by Urashan's long-time friend, Josh Hauser. (See page 267 entry.)

272 "Rilke" refers to the Bohemian-Austrian poet Rainer Maria Rilke, widely recognized as one of the most lyrically intense and inherently mystical German-language poets.

274 "I am being carried by the wind across the sky, I know not where" alludes to the Ojibwe passage referred to on page 213.

282 The Siskiyou Mountains, located in northwestern California and southwestern Oregon, are a coastal subrange of the Klamath Mountains. (See page 129 entry.)

285 Kali, also referred to as the Divine Mother or the Mother of the Universe, is a Hindu goddess; she is the destroyer of evil forces. The name Kali derived from the feminine form of "time" or "the fullness of time," and by extension, time as the "changing aspect of nature that bring things to life or death."

299 *Officium*, a 1994 album by Norwegian saxophonist Jan Garbarek and early music vocal group The Hilliard Ensemble, was recorded at the monastery of Propstei St. Gerold in Austria. The album starts and ends with music by the sixteenth-century Spanish composer Cristobal de Morales. The first song, "Parce mihi domine," is Italian for "Forgive me lord." "Officium" is a Latin word with various meanings in ancient Rome, including "service," "(sense of) duty," "courtesy," and "ceremony." "Office of the Dead" is a prayer cycle of the Canonical Hours in the Catholic Church, Anglican Church, and Lutheran Church, said for the repose of the soul of a decedent. [garbarek.com]

300 The Dark Rift—an area of dark bands that appear to obscure the center of the Milky Way galaxy when seen from the earth—are thought to be an aggregation of overlapping, non-luminous, molecular dust clouds that lie between the Solar System and the Sagittarius Arm of the galaxy. These clouds—estimated to contain about one million solar masses of plasma and dust—form a dark lane through the starry path of the Milky Way which, seen from Earth, is a hazy band of white light arching across the night sky.

305 "Sun-stand-still" refers to *solstice* which is derived from the Latin *sol* ("sun") and *sistere* ("to stand still"), because at the solstices the sun's declination appears to "stand still" when the seasonal movement of the sun's daily path (as seen from Earth) stops at its northern or southern limit before reversing direction.

308 The balsamic moon phase comes each month at the end of the lunar cycle, during the waning three and a half days right before the new moon. The balsamic moon is said to relate to one's commitment to destiny, so whenever the moon is in this position attention should be made to the earthly events that occur during this time. The balsamic moon also relates to healing and rest since it is the last phase before the new moon.

318 *Elizabeth.* Directed by Shekhar Kapur, starring Cate Blanchett in the title role of Queen Elizabeth I of England, Gramercy Pictures, 1998.

320 Mount Constance is the most visually prominent peak in the Olympic Mountains of Washington and the third highest in the range. Interestingly, despite being almost as tall as ice-clad Mount Olympus to the west, Mount Constance has little in the way of glaciers and permanent snow. However, the narrow and steep Crystal Glacier still exists on the mountain's north face, shaded by the bulk of the main peak. (See "ice field" allusions on pp 279-80, 299, and 323.) [peakvisor.com/peak/mount-constance.html]

320 See page 305 entry about "sun-stand-still."

327 Nepenthe—"that which chases away sorrow"—is a potion used by the ancients to induce forgetfulness of pain or sorrow; it is mentioned in Homer's *Odyssey* as banishing grief or trouble from a person's mind. It refers to any drug or potion bringing welcome forgetfulness.

330 Pope John Paul II's funeral brought together what was, at the time, the single largest gathering in history of heads of state outside the United Nations. Four kings, five queens, at least seventy presidents and prime ministers, and more than fourteen leaders of other religions attended, alongside the faithful. It is likely to have been one of the largest single gatherings of Christianity in history, with numbers estimated in excess of four million mourners gathering in Rome alone. Coinciding with the funeral in Vatican City, bishops at cathedrals throughout the world celebrated memorial masses. In an historical rarity, Protestant and Eastern Orthodox leaders, as well as representatives and heads from Judaism, Islam, and Buddhism, offered their own memorials and prayers as a way of sympathizing with the grief of Catholics. At the funeral itself, Ecumenical Patriarch Bartholomew I of the Eastern Orthodox Church was in the honorary first seat in the sector reserved for delegations from churches not in full communion with the See of Rome; this was the first time an Ecumenical Patriarch attended a papal funeral since the East–West Schism. The Archbishop of Canterbury (then Rowan Williams), was also present at the papal funeral, the first time since the Church of England broke with the Catholic Church in the 16th century. Also for the first time ever, the head of the Ethiopian Orthodox Tewahedo Church, Patriarch Abune Paulos, attended a papal funeral. [theperfectexposuregallery.com/exhibit/an-online-exhibit-the-funeral-of-pope-john-paul-ii]

330 "Miserere" (full title: "Miserere mei, Deus,"—Latin for "Have mercy on me, O God") is a musical setting of Psalm 51 by Italian composer Gregorio Allegri. It was composed during the reign of Pope Urban VIII, probably during the 1630s, for use in the Sistine Chapel during matins (a canonical hour of predawn prayer) and as part of the exclusive Tenebrae service on Holy Wednesday and Good Friday of Holy Week. [sin80.com/en/work/allegri-miserere]

330 The Litany of the Saints (Latin: Litaniae Sanctorum) is a formal prayer of the Roman Catholic Church as well as the Old Catholic Church, Anglo-Catholic communities, and Western Rite Orthodox communities. It is a prayer to the Triune God, which also includes invocations for the intercession of the Blessed Virgin Mary, the Angels and all the martyrs and saints upon whom Christianity was founded, and those recognized as saints through the subsequent history of the church. Following the invocation of the saints, the Litany concludes with a series of supplications to God to hear the prayers of the worshippers. It is most prominently sung during the Easter Vigil, All Saints' Day, and in the liturgy for conferring Holy Orders. [itmonline.org/bodytheology/litany.htm]

333 Bodhisattvas—Buddhist deities who have attained the highest level of enlightenment—delay their transcendence to help the earthbound. They usually appear as angels or take on the forms of other winged beings (such as the eagles on page 335). Bodhisattvas are powerful spiritual beings, able to act in seeming miraculous ways, and are associated with the qualities of compassion, wisdom, and mercy. [historytoday.com/archive/foundations/what-bodhisattva]

333 See page 185 entry for information on Leon Fleisher.

335 See page 13 entry about "Maris Stella."

339 In Greek mythology, Lethe is one of the five rivers of the underworld of Hades. It is also known as the Ameles potamos (the river of unmindfulness). The Lethe flowed around the cave of Hypnos and through the Underworld, where all those who drank from it experienced complete forgetfulness. Lethe was also the name of the Greek Goddess of Forgetfulness and Oblivion, with whom the river was often identified. In Classical Greek, the word "lethe" means "oblivion," "forgetfulness," or "concealment."

342 See page 102 entry about the City of Langley.

342 Susan Seddon Boulet was a noted San Francisco Bay Area artist who drew her inspiration from a wide variety of sources: mythology, poetry, Jungian psychology, and worldwide spiritual traditions, as well as a deep love of animals and the natural world. There is a fairy tale quality to her work, a sentimental recalling of childhood dreams of fairies and castles and magic. Working primarily in French oil pastels, inks, and occasionally pencil, Boulet developed a distinctive personal style characterized by the use of color applied in layers from which dream-like anthropomorphic images of animals, Shamans, and Goddesses emerged. She is considered one of the founders of the visionary art movement in the United States. [turningpointgallery.com/bio.asp]

342 See page 13 entry about "Maris Stella."

346 The scientist referred to here is Candace Beebe Pert, an American neuroscientist and pharmacologist who discovered the opiate receptor, the cellular binding site for endorphins in the brain. She is the author of *Molecules of Emotion: The Science Behind Mind-Body Medicine,* from which this passage is paraphrased.

350 The poet being paraphrased here is Joy Harjo, a member of the Muscogee Creek Nation and the first Native American U.S. Poet Laureate (2019-2021). From a June 19, 2019 interview with Harjo: npr.org/2019/06/19/733727917/joy-harjo-becomes-the-first-native-american-u-s-poet-laureate.

355 The lines cited here are from the poem "This Morning I Pray for My Enemies" by Joy Harjo. [Harjo, Joy, *Conflict Resolution for Holy Beings: Poems;* Copyright © 2015 by W. W. Norton & Company.]

356 See page 173 entry about the myth of Orpheus.

356 *Black Orpheus* is a modern cinematic retelling of the Orpheus and Eurydice myth (see page 173 entry) set at the annual Carnival in Rio de Janeiro. (*Black Orpheus.* Directed by Marcel Camus. GAGA Communications, France, 1959.)

357 The book of poetry alluded to here is *American Sonnets for My Past and Future Assassin* by Terrance Hayes. [terrancehayes.com]

359 Psalm 90:14

364 Daphne is a naiad (female nymph) associated with fountains, wells, springs, streams, brooks, and other bodies of freshwater. Due to a curse made by Eros, son of Venus, on Apollo, Daphne became the unwilling object of Apollo's infatuation; he chases her and just as he is about to catch up with Daphne, she pleads to her mother, Gaia, to save her; Gaia responds by transforming Daphne into a laurel tree. *Apollo and Daphne* is a larger than life Baroque marble sculpture by Italian artist Gian Lorenzo Bernini, finalized in 1625. [artble.com/artists/gian_lorenzo_bernini/sculpture/apollo_and_daphne]

367 Dale Chihuly is a Seattle-based glass sculptor and entrepreneur. His works are considered to possess outstanding artistic merit in the field of blown glass. The technical difficulties of working with glass forms are considerable, yet Chihuly uses it as the primary medium for his ethereal installations and environmental artwork. [chihuly.com]

367 Kew Gardens is a botanic garden in southwest London that houses the largest and most diverse botanical and mycological collections in the world. *Gardens of Glass: Chihuly at Kew* (2005) was the first outdoor exhibition in the UK by the renowned artist. This spectacular sequence of uniquely shaped and vibrantly colored installations set throughout Kew's 300-acre garden landscape was also the first exhibition of its kind in Europe. [kew.org]

373 The Christian holy day of Pentecost, which is celebrated fifty days from (including) Easter Sunday, commemorates the descent of the Holy Spirit ("tongues of fire") upon the Apostles while they were in Jerusalem celebrating the Feast of Weeks, as described in the Acts of the Apostles (Acts 2:1–31). Veni, Sancte Spiritus (Come, Holy Spirit) is a traditional prayer asking for the grace of the Holy Spirit. It has been used for centuries as a prayer of private devotion. The texts appear in the propers for the feast of Pentecost in both the Mass and Divine Office, and also in the votive Mass of the Holy Spirit. The season after Pentecost—also called Ordinary Time (see page 1 entry about "the sacred ordinary")—begins the day after Pentecost and ends the day before the First Sunday of Advent.

Photographs

As with the Notes, in order to preserve the writing as an uninterrupted whole, these photographs are displayed here as an appendix for those who might enjoy visuals of some of the places and descriptions in *The Sacred Ordinary*, as well as, of course, photos of the author herself through the years.

Maris Stella: Star of the Sea

Maris Stella: a house of joy, a place for contemplation. Casual, elegant, simple, it is all about the sea, the mountains, water, light. Hexagons, angles, sharp corners, tilted roofs, glass everywhere looking out. Strong intersecting lines, great black beams, open space with no ceilings, stone tile. And cedar! Cedar everywhere. (p 19)

So there we all are, so full of hope and glory, gathered around my grandmother's old oak table, with the Advent wreath, candles ablaze, still singing our hearts out on that yellowed newspaper now more than five decades old. (p 25)

My grandfather's buildings, which I know from a photograph, were a cluster of small shelters with shining windows and tent-like canvas roofs surrounding a deck, with a plank to the beach. (p 61)

The two young women are Mercedes, my not-yet-mother, and Florence, her younger sister. This was just before the start of WWI. (p 61)

My amazed mother happily welcomed a small 5½ pound, perfectly formed, bald-headed, blue-eyed baby girl—me—on May 17, 1927. (p 74)

*Hey Mom,
Can you see me
now? I'm here, with
my Goddess self. I
love you. I hope
you're happy.*

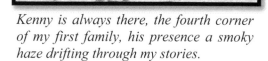

*Kenny is always there, the fourth corner
of my first family, his presence a smoky
haze drifting through my stories.*

Designed to keep sawing to a minimum, the cabin my dad built in 1933 was twenty-four-feet long, the length of the lumber. It had windows on either side of a sturdy front door, with a porch across the front. (p 56)

A few years later, my dad added on a kitchen wing and a workroom, expanding the old kitchen into the front bedroom. (p 56)

The kitchen at Camp after the remodel. (p 56)

A gift from my Grandma Cassia that she brought back after her trip to the Orient with Grandpa Robert. I kept wearing it year after year at the Maxwelton Parade, long after it became too small for me. (p 62)

My last clear memory of child-hood is pretend-sleeping on the forest floor with Hansel while the choir sings in high, clear voices that ethereal lullaby of guardian angels. (p 124)

*This is the outfit my mom made for me when I conducted my
first orchestra at Roosevelt High School when I was 15. (p 136)*

I graduated from the university. I did it with honors and my mother's Phi Beta Kappa key, but there was no joy, no honor. Just freedom. (p 142)

Skiing at Snoqualmie. (p 142)

In that first dance, the Introduction, no one is singing yet—the myth is but a gossamer hint; there are a mere handful of instruments; there are only two dancers; it is all just the beginning of an idea. (p 174)

Life was moving in an entirely new direction. I was a composer! (p 174)

On my own in Arcata, my old life vanished. (p 225)

And I go on writing Tropos. (p 225)

The beauty of this place grips and holds me close to the Goddess source.
The moon is waxing and I'll be here until she comes again. (pp 232-235)

Here, on the island, I have come home.
I won't leave again. (p 271)

My life has been heavy and harsh and I have been
depressed often and long. Yet I have looked up. ...
After the pain and rage heal, I know I have had a
magnificent life. ... I am being carried by the wind
across the sky, I know not where. (pp 273-289)